U.S. NAVY FIGHTERS OF WWII

Barrett Tillman and Robert L. Lawson

MBI Publishing Company

DEDICATION
Dedicated to the late Jeff Ethell: airman, colleague, friend.

ACKNOWLEDGMENTS
Hal Andrews, CAPT Ed Baumann, Bell Aircraft, Boeing Aircraft, CAPT I.F. Brown, USN(Ret), Bob Carlisle, Tom Doll, Harry Gann, Grumman Aircraft, Richard M. Hill Collection, Lois Lovisolo, Chuck McCandless, Jay Miller, Don W. Monson, Don Montgomery, Doug Olson, CAPT John A. Overn, Pete Peterson, Stan Piet, Herman L. Schonenberg, Ryan Aircraft, LCDR Tom Twomey, U.S. Navy ChInfo Photo Office, National Air and Space Museum

First published in 1998 by Motorbooks International Publishers & Wholesalers, PO Box 1, 729 Prospect Avenue, Osceola, WI 54020 USA

© Barrett Tillman and Robert L. Lawson, 1998.

MBI Publishing Company books are also available at discounts in bulk quantity for industrial or sales-promotional use. For details write to Special Sales Manager at Motorbooks International Wholesalers & Distributors, PO Box 1, 729 Prospect Avenue, Osceola, WI 54020 USA.

On the front cover: Factory-fresh F6F-3 models sported the red-outlined national insignia of summer 1943 and three-toned blue, gray, white paint. *Rudy Arnold, courtesy Stan Piet*

On the back cover: Corsairs produced their share of aces—most being land-based Marines during the island-hopping campaigns of the Pacific. 1st Lt. Jeremiah J. O'Keefe beams as he indicates his score of seven victories in his F4U-1D during May 1945 on Okinawa. O'Keefe became an "ace in a day" when he downed five Val kamikazes on 22 April. *USMC, Beall, courtesy Don Montgomery*

On the title page: TBF-1 Avenger comes aboard USS *Saratoga* (CV-3) as VF-12 F6F-3s are positioned forward near open elevator well. *USN, courtesy CHINFO Still Photo Office*

On the frontispiece: "The Forgotten Men" are the landing signal officers who brought the Navy's combat pilots and air crew safely back aboard the carriers. USS *Lexington* (CV-16) LSO, Ltjg. "Bud" Deering, guides a plane aboard Lex during the Marshalls and Gilberts operations, c. November 1943. Assistant LSO, Lt. Butler, observes from behind. *USN, courtesy CHINFO Still Photo Office*

Library of Congress Cataloging-in-Publication Data

Tillman, Barrett.
    U.S. Navy fighters of World War II./ Barrett Tillman & Robert L. Lawson.
        p.   cm. -- (Enthusiast color series)
      Includes index.
      ISBN 0-7603-0559-5
      1. Fighter planess--United States. 2. World War, 1939-1945--Aerial operations, American. 3. United States. Navy--Aviation--History. I. Lawson, Robert L. II. Title. III. Series.
    UG1242.F5T556 1998
    940. 54'4973--dc21   98-3915

Edited by Mike Haenggi
Designed by Katie L. Somnor

Printed in Hong Kong through World Print, Ltd.

Contents

Navy Fighter Organization

During the Second World War, the primary mission of U.S. Navy "fighting squadrons" (officially changed to "fighter squadrons" in 1948) was to keep aircraft carriers afloat. That vital task expanded drastically from 1942 to 1945, eventually forcing a 300 percent increase in the number of fighters embarked in a typical carrier.

To perform the role of fleet air defense and numerous related tasks, the United States Navy and Marine Corps flew three main fighter types during the war: the Grumman F4F Wildcat with its Eastern Aircraft FM variant; the Grumman F6F Hellcat; and the Vought F4U Corsair, also built by Goodyear and Brewster. Another Brewster entry, the F2A Buffalo, was produced in small numbers from 1938 to 1940 and found only limited combat at Midway. Subsequent Grumman wartime designs, the F7F Tigercat

Hellcats and Corsairs dominated NAAS Oceana's flight line near the end of World War II. At the end of the war, the Navy had more than 29,000 combat aircraft on inventory. *Author collection*

and F8F Bearcat, served well past 1945 but never fought the Empire of Japan.

By comparison, the U.S. Army Air Force operated five significant fighter types (P-38, -39, -40, -47, -51) and two lesser models (P-61 and -63) plus the British Spitfire and Beaufighter. In much smaller numbers the USAAF also used the obsolete P-35 and -36 in the war's earliest days, and the A-20 to P-70 night fighter conversion for a whopping total of 12 combat fighters.

Regardless of the number of types of fighters used, America's naval air force had to make up a serious deficit in both quality and quantity. In December 1941, the Navy possessed 131 front-line fighter aircraft in nine fleet squadrons aboard the seven aircraft carriers of the Atlantic and Pacific fleets. The Marine Corps had another 61 fighters in four squadrons from the East Coast to Hawaii.

7

Grumman's F4F Wildcat was just beginning fleet service as the Navy's primary fighter when the United States entered World War II. F4F-4 is on a Navy acceptance flight out of Grumman's Bethpage, Long Island, facility in late 1942 or early 1943. *Grumman, courtesy H.L. Schonenberg*

F6F-3 Hellcats began relieving the outclassed but capable Wildcats in the fleet during spring 1943 and were in combat by midsummer. Grumman F6F-3 wears the short-lived red surround national insignia in use June to September 1943. *Grumman, courtesy H.L. Schonenberg*

During 1941–1942 the Navy and Marine Corps flew identical aircraft: primarily Grumman F4F-3 or -3A Wildcats, but each still had a squadron of Brewster F2A-3 Buffalos. The era of biplane fighters had only just ended when two Marine squadrons exchanged their F3F-2s for Wildcats at the end of October 1941.

While the four Marine fighting squadrons were up to strength and a bit more, the carrier units faced a serious deficit: less than half their authorized aircraft. Eventually production on the home front narrowed the gap, but there were seldom notable surpluses of fighters in the year after Pearl Harbor. Indeed, when USS *Yorktown* (CV-5), *Enterprise* (CV-6),

Although initially flown 29 May 1940, Vought's F4U Corsair became a late entry in the war and first served in combat land-based with the Marines in the Solomons during February 1943. F4U-1 shows early style "birdcage" canopy in this 1943 photo. *Author collection*

Selected in 1938 over the F4F to be the Navy's primary carrier fighter, Brewster's F2A Buffalo failed as a carrier plane and had a limited service life; it was replaced by the Wildcat by early 1942. F2A-1 in 1941 overall gray paint scheme on a factory flight. *Author collection*

Dominating U.S. Navy fighter production for decades, Grumman next produced the F7F Tigercat. However, the F7F did not succeed as a carrier fighter but was used extensively by the Marines in night fighter and photo recon roles after World War II. F7F-3 wearing last three digits of its bureau number ("ferry numbers") is out of Bethpage c. early 1945. *Grumman, courtesy Lois Lovisolo*

Arguably the best piston-engined fighter ever produced in the world, Grumman's F8F Bearcat didn't make it to the fleet in time for World War II combat. Unidentified F8F-1 in flight 30 August 1945. *USN, courtesy Don Montgomery*

and *Hornet* (CV-8) sailed for the pivotal Battle of Midway in June 1942, there were virtually no spare F4F-4s to be found west of San Diego.

In September 1939, the month that World War II began in Europe, the U.S. Navy's new pilot training syllabus consisted of a six-month course in primary, basic, and advanced phases totaling 207 flying hours. Previously, it took a full year and some 300 hours to produce a "nugget" aviator for the fleet. Of the 6,500 naval aviators on duty at the time of Pearl Harbor (including Marine and Coast Guard pilots), nearly half were reservists. They included numerous Naval Aviation Pilots—noncommissioned fliers who filled the cockpits of fighters and torpedo planes in the fleet as well as patrol, transport, and utility aircraft elsewhere.

A 1985 survey produced some illuminating data on the experience level of World War II combat pilots. The average total flight time of Navy and Marine fighter aces flying their first combat mission was a whopping 805 hours. The figure probably is skewed somewhat by the fact that prewar aviators with greater experience

"made ace" in 1942–43, whereas, from 1944 onward, the streamlined Training Command produced quality fliers with somewhat less flight time. Still, those wearing wings of gold enjoyed a substantial advantage over most of the Army Air Force aces, who averaged 600 hours upon entering combat.

Another major factor in the success of Navy and Marine fighter squadrons was the institutional emphasis on gunnery. In fact, the same aces poll showed naval aviators most confident in gunnery while Army aces considered their strength to be total flight time. Before World War II, the U.S. Navy and the Finnish Air Force apparently were the only air arms that stressed deflection shooting. This institutional dedication to wide-angle gunnery spelled the difference between success and failure, especially in the crucial first year of the Pacific War, when the Japanese Navy possessed aircraft of superior performance.

Throughout the war, most Navy carrier squadrons were led by a lieutenant commander while Marine outfits were usually headed by the

The finale of Navy/Marine Corps biplane fighters came two months prior to America's entry into World War II as the last two Marine squadrons traded their Grumman F3F-2s for Wildcats. VF-5 F3F-2s in standard three-plane fighter section during a spring 1939 flight off So. California. Red tails show VF-5s assignment to USS *Yorktown* (CV-5). *USN, courtesy Don Montgomery*

Boeing's F4B was that company's last fighter produced for the Navy. The F4B was in fleet service 1929–1937, but continued in training command and utility roles until 1942. NAS Miami F4B-3 (#55) and F4B-4s on late 1930s training flight. *Author collection*

equivalent rank of major. The main exceptions occurred during 1942 when Navy lieutenants (equal to Marine or Army captains) occasionally became the senior officer, sometimes for a period of months. In descending order, the hierarchy was executive officer (XO) and flight (operations) officer, followed by the various department heads. A half century after the war a former F6F pilot, retired Rear Adm. Jack Christiansen, joked, "I think that the ideal rank was lieutenant (junior grade). You were too senior for the chief petty officers to beat up on you, and too junior for any real responsibility!"

At the start of World War II in 1939, most Navy fighter squadrons employed a tactical organization based on three-plane sections: a leader and two wingmen. Two sections comprised a six-plane division with nominally three divisions per squadron. However, two-plane sections were tested by at least two squadrons: VF-2 aboard *Lexington* (CV-2) and VF-5 assigned to *Yorktown* (CV-5). Trials had proven the superiority of four-plane divisions, with greater flexibility and the prospect for bringing more firepower to bear, despite fewer aircraft. The reason was simple: a three-plane "vic" or inverted V often allowed only the leader to shoot, as his two wingmen were equally

Student pilot prepares for flight in an F3F-1 at NAS Miami c. 1941 as plane captain stands by for engine start. *Courtesy Stan Piet*

Early war carrier air groups placed emphasis on dive-bombing and torpedo planes as evidenced by CVG-9 in this fall 1943 photo of VF-9 F6F-3s and VB/VS-9 SBD-3s on board USS *Essex* (CV-9). *USN, courtesy Bob Carlisle*

concerned with keeping formation or watching one another's tails. In pairs, a 50 percent gain in shooters was possible with the same number of aircraft.

Trial and evaluation continued over the next several months, with favorable results. Despite a lapse on the part of Vice Admiral William F. Halsey, Commander of the Pacific Fleet's Air Battle Force, who prohibited the use of two-plane sections, the junior officers persisted. Eventually Halsey reversed himself, and during summer 1941 both the Pacific and Atlantic Fleet air commands authorized the more flexible formation.

During that last summer of peace in America, another junior leader was preparing for war. Lieutenant Commander John S. Thach, skipper of

Saratoga's (CV-3) Fighting Three, saw additional potential in the two-plane section. Already aware of the greater flexibility of fighting pairs, Thach exploited both the offensive and defensive potential. His solution involved leader and wingman flying abreast of one another, spaced so that their spread equaled a normal-radius turn at a given altitude and airspeed. If attacked from behind, a turn into one's partner forced the bogey to cross the guns of the unengaged fighter. Thach's "beam defense" worked equally well with two sections. Thus, the Thach Weave established the basis for the standard Navy (and eventually U.S. Air Force) fighter formation well into the jet age: the

By early 1944, Independence-class CVLs operated with only fighters and torpedo bombers in their air groups. By mid-1944, in time for the Marianas campaign, all air groups placed more emphasis on fighters. VF-22 F6F-3s ready for launch against the Marianas from USS *Cowpens* (CVL-25) c. July 1944. *USN, courtesy Don Montgomery.*

"loose deuce" spread. Additionally, lookout doctrine was improved by easing the need for two wingmen to maintain proper formation in the old three-plane V.

If there was one continuous trend in naval fighter aviation, it was insufficient numbers of aircraft aboard ship. At the start of the war the nominal complement for a fighter squadron, or "FitRon," was 18 airplanes. But early combat experience proved that number too few for both defensive patrols near the ship and escort of dive bombers and torpedo planes. Just before Midway the number was increased to 27, partly made possible by the advent of the folding-wing F4F-4. However, before year's

end most large carriers embarked 36 Wildcats: a 100 percent increase in roughly 10 months.

The use of three dozen fighters was more or less constant for big-deck carriers until early 1944, by which time the Independence class (CVL-22) ships were well established. Operating only fighters and torpedo planes, without dive bombers, the light carriers were incapable of packing as many planes into their cruiser hulls as the prewar and Essex class (CV-9) ships. Still, the numbers grew as the deficit in flight and hangar deck space was absorbed by "beaching" more and more TBF/TBM Avengers or SB2C Helldivers from the Essexes. A typical CVL air group embarked 24 Hellcats during 1943–44.

USS *Sangamon* (CVE-26) at anchor off a South Pacific island, c. 1943, is typical of the several escort carriers ("jeeps") that served in both the Atlantic and Pacific theaters. *USN, courtesy Don Montgomery*

By mid-1944, in time for the Marianas operation, most fast carriers had 35 to 40 fighters, including special-mission photo and night fighter aircraft. But that figure increased again in time for the Philippines operation: during the Battle of Leyte Gulf in October, CV-9 class carriers averaged about 54 Hellcats.

Even that increase was relatively short-lived, owing to the *kamikaze* crisis that accompanied the Philippines campaign. With fleet defense more important than ever, big-deck air groups disembarked as many as half their dive bombers and torpedo planes to make room for 73-plane fighter squadrons. In fact, early in 1945 the administrative workload of some 110 to 120 pilots for six dozen fighters resulted in splitting the FitRons. Generally, the CO retained the original organization with his exec taking half the roster to form a bombing-fighting (VBF) squadron. In most carriers, the two squadrons flew the same aircraft (invariably F6Fs) but some late-war air groups deployed with a mixed complement: Hellcat fighters and F4U Corsair fighter-bombers. Before VJ-Day, however, a few air groups' fighters were 100 percent Vought "U-Birds."

Corsairs only appeared in strength aboard U.S. Navy carriers in December 1944. Briefly caught at a numerical disadvantage owing to an optimistic reduction in pilot training, the Navy had too few fighter squadrons ready to counter the aerial suicide menace. Therefore, Marine F4U outfits were hastily "car-qualled" and sent to fill the breach—sometimes without benefit of full training in carrier operations or instrument flying. Casualties were heavy in the first several weeks, more to weather than combat, but eventually the Fly-ing Leathernecks became certified tailhook aviators, and began bagging their share of *kamikazes*.

In addition to the fast carriers (those capable of 30 knots) were scores of escort carriers or CVEs. Intended primarily as antisubmarine platforms, the "jeep carriers" performed prodigious work in both the Atlantic and Pacific, usually operating composite squadrons (VCs) of Grumman or Eastern Wildcats and Avengers. Though not strictly fighter squadrons, owing to the mixed nature of their calling, the CompRons nevertheless accounted for some 400 Axis aircraft shot down from 1943 through 1945. The fighter pilots in each VC were dedicated to the VF role, which included CAP, strike escort, and close air support. Five FM-2 pilots became aces while flying from CVEs, and one such unit—VOC-1 aboard *Wake Island* (CVE-65) and *Marcus Island* (CVE-77), probably logged more hours per pilot than any carrier squadron in 1945.

There were also CVE air groups, somewhat different organizationally from the more familiar VC squadrons. Escort carrier air groups followed the CVL pattern, with separate fighter and torpedo plane squadrons rather than mixing both types in a CompRon. The usual distinction was Hellcats in the VF outfit rather than Wildcats, though occasionally CVEGs did embark an FM-2 squadron. The reason for the difference possibly stems from the origin of those few squadrons within air groups that had not operated together before 1943.

A similar situation existed late in the war among Marine carrier air groups, which flew a mixture of F4Us and F6F special-mission aircraft plus a TBM squadron for heavy attack. Flying from escort carriers specifically devoted to support amphibious operations, the Leatherneck CVEGs filled a gap in air-ground coordination that had existed since the earliest days of the war.

Finally, at war's end, the ultimate in carrier air groups was realized in the *Midway* (CVB-41) class:

The ultimate in carrier air groups were the CVBGs designed to operate as many as 120 aircraft from the new Midway-class carriers commissioned in 1945, but too late for World War II combat. VF-75 F4U-4s on Leeward Point flight line at Guantanamo Bay, Cuba, in 1946, belong to CVBG-75 assigned to USS *Franklin D. Roosevelt* (CVB-42). *Capt. Don W. Monson*

huge 120-plane air groups with as many as six squadrons, including four Corsair outfits.

Despite most of the headlines, and the greatest share of the history, naval fighters also played a major role in the land-based air war. It was especially true of Marine Corps squadrons, first at Wake Island, then at Midway, and most especially at Guadalcanal and other islands farther up the Solomons chain. Tactically there was no difference in the way land-based FitRons operated and their

carrier-borne cousins, as command structure and division organization were identical.

The main difference usually was found in maintenance. Whereas most embarked squadrons relied mainly upon the ship's carrier air service detachment (CASD), land-based units generally had organic maintenance departments under a specialist engineering officer with petty officers and enlisted men dedicated to handle engine, airframe, ordnance, and related matters.

Some exceptions to the foregoing rule existed in the Solomon Islands during 1943–44. Ordinarily, pilots rotated in and out of the combat area for six-week periods with one or two weeks of rest and recreation in between. However, squadron maintenance personnel seldom enjoyed that luxury. Owing to a pressing need for all available aircraft at any given time, squadrons whose pilots were on R and R frequently had their airplanes assigned to a pool whose assets could be allocated where needed. Consequently, those fighters sometimes received little more than daily inspections because they were not "owned" by a specific unit in that period. When the air echelon returned to the combat area, many of its planes might badly need deferred maintenance such as periodic inspections, engine changes, or replacement of major components.

Apparently the problem was far less severe during the Okinawa campaign of 1945. By then, enough aircraft, spares, and mechanics were available so that unit-level maintenance was largely accomplished within the squadron. Depot-level maintenance beyond that performed in a squadron (major rebuilds or repair of extensive battle damage) was more often done by centralized pools administered at the group or wing level.

Night fighter units had their own special requirements. Generally they were smaller than standard squadrons and, as a rule, more often operated as detachments when aboard ship but as squadrons when ashore. Other than the obvious need for specialists in radar maintenance and operation, VF(N) organizations also required close coordination with fighter directors whether at sea or ashore.

From early 1944 until the Leyte Gulf battle that fall, three Navy night fighter squadrons operated with the fast carriers with four-plane detachments assigned to each big-deck ship. However, in October-November, most were absorbed into the resident air group, operating as part of the normal fighter squadron. The first dedicated night air group went aboard *Independence* (CVL-22) in August and remained until January 1945, being followed by three more specialist air groups, each with a fighter (F6F) and torpedo bomber (TBM) squadron.

Eventually three Marine F6F night fighter squadrons flew from Okinawa, being fully self-contained for nocturnal operations and maintenance, while another was based in the Philippines.

Maintenance of carrier-based squadrons was performed by the ship's carrier air service detachment (CASD), while land-based units generally had organic maintenance departments. Aviation machinist mates work on a Corsair's Pratt and Whitney R-2800 engine. *USN, courtesy Don Montgomery*

CHAPTER 2

Grumman F4F Wildcat

The importance of Grumman Aircraft Engineering Corporation to carrier aviation can hardly be overstated. From the biplane FF-1 of 1931 to the variable sweep-wing F-14D of the 1990s, "Grumman" and "Navy fighter" have been almost synonymous. At the height of World War II, during the Marianas campaign of June 1944, nearly 80 percent of the embarked carrier aircraft—fighters and bombers— were either designed or built by the Long Island firm.

Though Grumman's biplane fighters had been commercially and operationally successful, by the mid-1930s the global trend was clear: monoplanes owned the future. In fact, as of 1933 the Army Air Corps was committed to monoplane fighters, bombers, and attack aircraft while the Navy had yet to field a similar type.

Other firms already had produced all-metal, mono-

plane fighters for Navy consideration: Boeing, Curtiss, and Northrop. A variety of problems prevented their production, including excessively high speeds in the crucial carrier landing pattern. But European developments forced the Bureau of Aeronautics to seek more modern aircraft. Therefore, prototypes were ordered from Brewster and Grumman in 1936, leading to the XF2A-1 (later Buffalo) and XF4F-1(later Wildcat).

Eventually the Brewster design was selected, with 54 production "dash ones" ordered in June 1938, though most went to Finland. In all, the U.S. Navy procured 163 Buffalos through the end of 1941. The F2A's primary failing was poor carrier suitability—so much so that the only fleet squadron, *Lexington's* VF-2, grounded its Buffalos immediately before Pearl Harbor in order to retain some operational fighters if war broke out.

Lack of two-stage R-1830-76 supercharged engines led to installation of Pratt and Whitney's single-stage Wasp R-1830-90 radials with two-speed superchargers in the 95 F4F-3A Wildcats. VF-8 F4F-3As over South Carolina during August 1941 war games in "Orange Forces" markings.

23

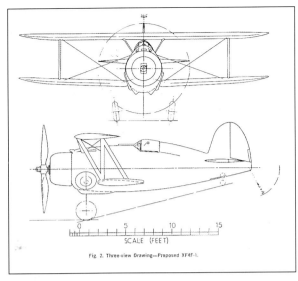

Design drawing of the proposed XF4F-1 shows original biplane concept. *Courtesy Grumman History Center*

The Navy's dual procurement policy was never better illustrated than when the Grumman design was also selected for production. Originally drafted as another biplane, the XF4F-1 was quickly redesigned as a monoplane to compete with the Brewster, and the XF4F-2 first flew in September 1937. As with so many Grumman designs, the original test pilot was Robert Hall, who had helped design the fabulous GeeBee racers. The Navy requested several modifications, including a redesigned wing and empennage, and more powerful Pratt and Whitney R-1830 engine. Consequently, in August 1939, an initial production order was placed for 54 production "dash threes."

At the same time, foreign air arms were seriously interested in the new Grumman. Factory model G-36A (XF4F-5) won the attention of the French Navy, which ordered 81 fighters powered by Wright R-1820 Cyclones. Ironically, the first G-36A cranked its wheels into the well on 11 May 1940, the day after

The first monoplane fighter built by Grumman was the F4F Wildcat, which began as a biplane design but was revamped to catch up with state-of-the-art fighters of the late 1930s. Second production F4F-3 BuNo 1845 on a test flight over Long Island during 1940. *Rudy Arnold, courtesy Hal Andrews*

German troops entered Paris. But the British Royal Navy quickly absorbed the *Aeronavale* fighters and placed them into service as Martlet Mark Is. Little time was lost putting them to use: a pair of land-based Martlets flying from the Orkney Islands shot down a snooping Junkers 88 bomber on Christmas Day, 1940.

That same month the first American fleet squadron received its initial F4F-3s. Fighting Four aboard USS *Ranger* (VF-4) at Norfolk, Virginia, inaugurated the new Grumman to U.S. service with the standard configuration: a 1,200-horsepower R-1830-76 P&W radial with four 50 caliber machine guns in the "stiff" (nonfolding) wing. The Navy wanted nearly as many F4Fs as Grumman could produce, but lacked enough two-stage, supercharged aircraft engines. Therefore, Pratt and Whitney's single-stage Wasp engine was substituted in the model originally called XF4F-6 but produced as the F4F-3A. One hundred similar fighters were delivered to the Royal Navy as Martlet IIs. The British shortly acquired 30 more intended for Greece in April 1941, when Germany and Italy occupied the Hellenic peninsula. Designated Martlet IIIs, they were quickly absorbed by the hard-pressed Fleet Air Arm, which still lacked an indigenous naval fighter of comparable design. One of the Fleet Air Arm's most notable aviators, later Captain Eric Brown, flew Martlets from an escort carrier in the North Atlantic and called the Wildcat derivative "The love of my life."

Little recalled today is the British influence on subsequent Wildcat design. The Royal Navy had already requested a six-gun fighter, which Grumman provided in a trial batch of 10 Mark IIs. The balance

Eighty-one G-36As (XF4F-5) were ordered by France in 1939, but were delivered to the British Royal Navy instead in July 1940 after the collapse of French forces. Named "Martlet I" by the British, this G-36A wears the British roundel insignia along with French rudder stripes. *Grumman, courtesy H.L. Schonenberg*

of the Mark II order was provided with folding wings, which led to the definitive Wildcat, the F4F-4.

The U.S. Navy already had expressed interest in the folding wing model, which first flew in April 1941. Deliveries to the fleet began in November, but the "dash four" Wildcat had to wait until the Battle of Midway in June 1942 to prove itself.

Pilot reaction to the F4F-4 was decidedly mixed. The new fighter was 460 pounds heavier "dry" than the dash three and consequently was slower on the level and in a climb. Perhaps more important, the folding

wing and six-gun armament allowed 250 rounds per gun (1,440 total) compared to the dash three's 450 rounds per four guns (1,800 total). Nevertheless, the dash four was the airplane that fought the Midway, Guadalcanal, and lower Solomons battles of 1942–43. The British version, Martlet Mark IV, had Wright R-1820s in place of the Pratt and Whitney R-1830. The one advantage was the folding wing, which reduced span from 38 feet to barely 14 and thereby allowed nearly twice the number of fighters for the same deck space.

Next up in the production sequence was the F4F-7, a photo reconnaissance aircraft stripped of guns and most other removable items, such as self-sealing fuel tanks. The 21 dash sevens were doled out to fleet carriers and Marine air groups at the rate of one or two each, and were little used in combat. However, their potential was considerable, with cameras mounted in

U.S. Navy deliveries of the F4F-3 Wildcat began in December 1940 following acceptance by Britain's Fleet Air Arm of the Martlet I version of the G-36A in July. VF-42 F4F-3 BuNo 2526 is in flight during February 1941. The aircraft wears the Willow Green tail color of USS *Ranger* (CV-4) but does not yet have the squadron markings applied to the fuselage. *Courtesy Richard M. Hill*

The definitive version of the Wildcat was the F4F-4 with six 50-caliber guns in its folding wings. *Author collection*

the belly and 685 gallons of internal fuel, which equated to a mission *radius* of more than 1,500 miles.

In keeping with the global nature of the war, the Wildcat's first day of combat in American hands occurred simultaneously on 7 and 8 December 1941—both sides of the International Date Line. Marine Fighting Squadron 211 began its valiant defense of Wake Island and *Enterprise's* VF-6 lost three pilots trying to land at Pearl Harbor that evening.

Beginning in February, American carriers were committed to a series of hit-and-run raids against Japanese bases in the Central and Southwest Pacific. Combat experience demonstrated a growing need for increased fighter strength, resulting in production of the F4F-4, the ultimate variant of the Grumman Wildcat. With folding

wings and six .50 caliber guns, the dash four became the most-produced model of Wildcat, with 1,389 delivered to the U.S. Navy, Marine Corps, and Royal Navy during 1941 and 1942. By the Battle of Midway in June 1942, each PacFleet FitRon embarked 27 rather than 18 Wildcats. But even that number was deemed insufficient. By fall the standard VF complement was 36 F4Fs, a figure that remained relatively constant into early 1944.

However, the F4F-4 was not without its drawbacks. With no additional power from its R-1830 engine, the new fighter was slower to climb than the dash three series, with less service ceiling. Additionally, the folding wing and placement of two extra guns reduced the Wildcat's ammunition capacity by 360 rounds, or 20 percent. In the Santa Cruz

New features of the F4F-4 created more weight with resultant reduction of performance and ammunition capacity. Wartime-censored photo has eliminated VF-41 markings from the fuselage and gun ports from the wings of this F4F-4 in flight c. 1942. *Rudy Arnold, courtesy Grumman History Center*

engagement of October 1942, *Enterprise* and *Hornet* pilots experienced the frustration of circling near the task force with dozens of enemy aircraft in the vicinity but no remaining ammunition.

Though destined for glory in the Pacific, where eight Wildcat pilots received the Medal of Honor, the F4F also fought the western Axis. Five squadrons supported the allied landings in North Africa in November 1942, and 11 months later *Ranger's* VF-4 was involved in an antishipping strike above the Arctic Circle.

With demand increasing month by month, the Navy realized that Grumman could not continue building Wildcats as well as Avenger torpedo planes in addition to the new F6F Hellcat. Therefore, when

the 1,971st F4F model was delivered in May 1943, plans were already underway for an alternate source of Wildcats.

In April 1942, at the time of the Doolittle raid on Japan, the Navy contracted with Eastern Aircraft Division of General Motors Corporation to build duplicate F4F-4s under the designation FM-1. Except for the first 10 aircraft, the Eastern fighters were delivered with four 50 calibers, each with 430 rounds. The first flight from the Linden, New Jersey, plant was logged on 30 August at which time the fledgling Cactus Air Force was just spreading its wings at Guadalcanal. GM also produced TBM Avengers at nearby Trenton.

As a result of an overload of Grumman tactical aircraft World War II production capability, F4F Wildcats and TBF Avengers were built by the Eastern Aircraft Division of General Motors as FMs and TBMs. FM-2 version of the F4F-8, wearing Atlantic ASW paint scheme, taxis from the landing area of USS *Charger* (CVE-30) 8 May 1944. *USN, courtesy Don Montgomery*

With the arrival of escort carriers to the fleet in 1942, F4F-4s initially equipped their fighter components in both the European and Pacific theaters. F4F-4s of VGF-29 are awaiting launch preparations from USS *Santee* (ACV-29), c. late 1942. *USN, Author collection*

Of 1,150 FM-1s built during 1942–43, 311 went to Britain as Martlet Mark IVs. However, in spring 1944 the Royal Navy changed its names for Grumman aircraft, and Martlets became Wildcats just as Tarpons became Avengers.

In November 1942 Grumman had flown its ultimate Wildcat, the XF4F-8 with an R-1820 Wright engine, four machine guns, and a taller vertical stabilizer and rudder. The test pilot was Selden "Connie" Converse, logging the first flight in a Wildcat variant for at least the seventh time.

Eastern Aircraft became responsible for production of the dash eight, which emerged as the FM-2, fondly known as the "Wilder Wildcat." In 24 months, from September 1943 to August 1945, the Linden factory turned out 4,777 FM-2s—an average of 200 per month or nearly seven a day. Again the Royal Navy benefited from GM's production skill, receiving 340 Wildcat VIs.

The FM-2 became *the* CVE fighter, flying alongside TBM-3s from escort carriers in the Atlantic and Pacific. Capable of carrying two bombs and six rockets, the scrappy little "beer barrel on skates" made a reputation for effective close air support in numerous island campaigns and also helped blunt the German submarine menace.

At the end of the war in September 1945, Grumman had delivered 1,978 fighters of the G-36/F4F family (431 for Britain) while Eastern rolled out 5,927 (651 for Britain)—a grand total of 7,905. They had flown under eight different U.S. designations and six British marks.

Whatever its shortcomings, the F4F retained the priceless asset of availability. Whether operating from fleet carriers, ashore at Guadalcanal in the Solomon Islands, or from escort carriers hunting U-boats, it was there in sufficient strength. Perhaps the ultimate statement on the Wildcat came from no less an authority than Lieutenant Commander James Flatley, skipper of VF-10, who said, "Let us not be too critical of our equipment. It shoots the enemy down in flames and brings most of us home."

Little more could be demanded of any fighter aircraft.

31

Grumman F6F Hellcat

Three American aircraft made aviation's greatest influence on the Pacific War. Two were carrier planes; one was an Army Air Force strategic bomber. Among them, they spanned the 44 months from Pearl Harbor to Tokyo Bay.

The most spectacular, of course, was Boeing's B-29 Superfortress, the four-engined instrument of air power that not only delivered history's first atomic bombs but burned out hundreds of square miles of Japanese cities to cripple enemy industry in 1944–45.

Among those aircraft that held the line early in the war, then reversed an appalling string of Japanese victories, was the Douglas SBD Dauntless. The prewar scout-bomber, already slated for replacement in 1942, proved the decisive instrument of naval aviation in that crucial year.

Dauntless aircrews—and surely they were dauntless—gained historic victories at Coral Sea, Midway, and Guadalcanal. In fact, some SBD pilots such as Lieutenants S.W. "Swede" Vejtasa and William E. Henry went on to earn outstanding reputations in fighters and night fighters.

Between these two dissimilar types of bombers was the one fighter most responsible for destroying Japanese air power. Grumman's angular F6F Hellcat, successor to the Wildcat, was produced in prodigious numbers: more than 12,000 in less than three years.

By comparison, 10,000 Mitsubishi Zeros were built in nearly twice that time.

The bare statistics demonstrate the Hellcat's importance toward VJ-Day. Credited with 5,200 aerial victories and 306 aces—more than produced by any other U.S. fighter—the F6F led the Pacific hit parade by a wide

Destined to become the Navy's premier fighter of World War II, Grumman's F6F-3 Hellcat first entered fleet service on the East Coast 16 January 1943 in USS *Essex* (CV-9). VF-3, on the West Coast, had F6F-3s by April. F6F-3 of VF-3 or -9, over So. California during spring 1943.

Hellcats were used extensively in drone operations during and after the war as both control and target aircraft. F6F-3K drone in flight at top was used in the 1946 Operation Crossroads atomic bomb tests at Bikini Atoll in the Pacific. At bottom is an F6F-3K in World War II overall yellow drone scheme at NAMU Johnsville, Pennsylvania. *USN, courtesy Tom Doll; USN, Author collection*

margin. Aerial victories credited to American fighter squadrons in the Pacific Theater were:

F6F Hellcat	5,156*	306 aces
F4U Corsair	2,140	93 aces
P-38 Lightning	1,700	90 aces
F4F/FM Wildcat	1,006	58 aces
P-40 series	706	27 aces
P-47 Thunderbolt	697	32 aces
P-51 Mustang	296	5 aces
P-39 Airacobra	243	1 ace
P-61 Black Widow	63	1 ace
	12,007	706 aces

Some aviators are born fighter pilots. Lt. Stanley W. "Swede" Vejtasa proved this in a 40-minute fight against overwhelming odds at the Battle of Coral Sea 8 May 1942. Vejtasa was credited with three Zeros during the engagement, flying a VS-5 SBD-2 Dauntless from USS *Yorktown* (CV-5). Douglas SBD-5 is off Santa Monica during 1944. *Douglas, courtesy Harry Gann*

(includes those who "made ace" in two aircraft)
* Some F6F night fighter scores are unknown

These figures do not include nearly 1,500 shootdowns credited to the Army and Flying Tigers in the China-Burma-India theater, but even so, Hellcats claimed almost 40 percent of all Japanese aircraft

Pacific theater Hellcat pilots were credited with nearly 5,200 aerial victories, which produced 306 aces—more than any other U.S. fighter. Japanese Navy A6M3 Zero lies wrecked at Munda Air Field, New Georgia, Solomon Islands, in late 1943. *USN, courtesy Don Montgomery*

Carrier- and land-based Hellcat pilots scored victories in both Europe and the Pacific. Japanese G4M Betty bomber begins its descent to the bottom of the Pacific Ocean after succumbing to a U.S. attack. *USN, courtesy Don Montgomery*

destroyed in aerial combat by American fighters in World War II. With Wildcats and Corsairs, the Navy and Marine Corps, contribution exceeded 60 percent. Hellcats also produced nearly half of all American aces in the Pacific Theater. Clearly, the Grumman Hellcat was the worst enemy of Japanese air power.

In some ways the Hellcat was a bigger, better Wildcat. Navy fighter squadrons required more speed, better altitude performance, and especially more range; the F6F delivered in each area.

Contrary to myth and legend, the F6F was neither designed nor built specifically to counter the Mitsubishi Zero. The XF6F-1 prototype, with a Wright R-2600 engine, first flew on 26 June

1942, about three weeks after the fabled "Alaskan Zero" overturned during a forced landing in Attu's tundra during the diversionary portion of Japan's Midway operation. However, once recovered and flown by U.S. Navy aviators and engineers, the A6M2 was tested against Hellcats and other American fighters.

Grumman quickly ironed out the wrinkles in its new product. Entering production in late 1942 with Pratt and Whitney's wondrous R-2800 engine, the F6F-3 became the standard by which other naval fighters were measured. The pilots of Fighting Nine took first delivery amidst a snowstorm that December, enjoying the holiday season in the Big Apple

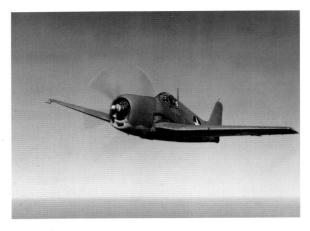

Design of the Hellcat began in late 1940, and, contrary to popular writings, the F6F was neither designed nor built specifically to counter the Mitsubishi Zero. F6F-3 comparison photos show the Hellcat in both "clean" and "dirty" flight configurations. *Rudy Arnold, courtesy Grumman History Center; USN, courtesy Bob Carlisle*

before returning to NAS Norfolk to begin learning their new weapon.

A factory technical representative described Roy Grumman's design philosophy: make an airplane that a 200-hour pilot could fly from a carrier, that was easy to maintain, that could be built in large numbers. Before long, the company was producing more aircraft in a week than Grumman had previously built in a year.

In order to handle the volume of production and experimental test work, Grumman scrounged pilots from any source possible. One of the fortunates involved in the F6F program was 22-year-old Corwin "Corky" Meyer, who in late 1942 was hired with 423 hours total flight time. The next week he was checked out in amphibians, torpedo planes, and fighters. As Bre'r Rabbit said, "Please don't throw me into dat briar patch!"

One of Meyer's early jobs was inverted spins in the Hellcat. None of the other factory pilots had been able to get the F6F into that unusual attitude, but Meyer found a way. Recovery was surprisingly easy. Not so easy were the three consecutive engine failures

he experienced when trying to qualify the new fighter for high altitude. When queried on the matter, Pratt & Whitney admitted that pressurized ignition harnesses were required above 32,000 feet. After that fix was installed, the F6F-3 climbed to 39,400 feet.

Today, Meyer insists that the conventional wisdom regarding the F6F and F4U is wrong. He found the Hellcat just as fast as the Corsair, despite specifications that show a 30-mile-per-hour advantage to the Vought. Meyer replies, "The bent-wing had a different pitot system than we did, and it gave different readings. But I can tell you that flying side by side, the F6 not only had as good a Vmax as the Corsair, it accelerated as well, too." Grumman found that the F4U's only advantage was 15 to 20 knots faster in "main blower stage" below 5,000 feet. Otherwise, performance was nearly identical—hardly surprising for two fighters with the same engine, propeller, and similar wingspans.

Explaining the F6F design philosophy, Roy Grumman said: "The Hellcat was designed so a 200-hour pilot had an excellent chance to take off from a carrier, fight successfully with the enemy, safely and

F6F-3s entered combat 31 August 1943 in attacks against Marcus Island. Flying from USS *Essex* (CV-9), *Yorktown* (CV-10), and *Independence* (CVL-22), Hellcats of VF-9, VF-5, and a detachment of VF-6 wrote the first page of a glorious history in fighter aviation. VF-1 (later VF-5) F6F-3 comes aboard *Yorktown* during her spring 1943 shakedown off Trinidad. *Lt. Charles Kerlee, courtesy Don Montgomery*

easily land aboard his carrier at night, even if he was shot up, and be able to fight again the next day."

Naval Aviators began doing just that as Hellcats entered combat during summer 1943. From shore bases in the Solomon Islands and from fast carriers in the Central Pacific, Hellcat squadrons began taking the fight to the Japanese. The F6F immediately replaced Wildcats on all big-deck carriers while F4Fs and FMs remained the primary escort carrier fighters for "the duration".

Early fighter pilot reaction to the new Grumman was enthusiastic and heartfelt. The first Hellcat ace

Early model F6F-3s of VF-5 ready for launch from USS *Yorktown* (CV-10) during fall 1943 combat operations in the Pacific. Red outlined national insignia have been partially replaced by blue outline under the wings, but not yet on fuselage. Blue outline replaced red officially in September 1943. *USN, courtesy CHINFO Still Photo Office*

Flight deck crewmen await to pull chocks from under a VF-1 F6F-3 prior to launch from USS *Yorktown* (CV-10) during spring 1943 shakedown cruise. *Lt. Charles Kerlee, courtesy CHINFO Still Photo Office*

and double ace was Lieutenant Hamilton McWhorter of VF-9, while his squadronmate, Lieutenant (jg) Gene Valencia, told a reporter, "I love this airplane so much that if it could cook, I'd marry it".

The F6F-3 proved itself a rugged, maintainable aircraft both afloat and ashore, with availability rates typically over 90 percent. The "dash three" won its greatest laurels during the Marianas campaign when the nine carriers of Task Force 58 repelled successive enemy carrier- and land-based attacks on 19 June 1944. At day's end, the Imperial Navy's carefully hoarded reserve of carrier aviators was depleted as F6F squadrons destroyed 300 or more Japanese planes. On that day alone, six Hell-

Fly One officer signals VF-5 pilot for full power just before launch from USS *Yorktown* (CV-10) c. late 1943-early 1944. Air Group Five served in *Yorktown* from April 1943 until May 1944. *Lcdr. Charles Kerlee, courtesy CHINFO Still Photo Office*

Red-capped ordnancemen rearm F6F-5 Hellcats aboard a carrier c. 1944–1945. Overall glossy sea-blue-painted F6F-5s began fleet service in late 1944. All known photographs of F6Fs in the combat area in all-blue paint are -5s; it is doubtful that any F6F-3s were repainted to conform to the September 1944 directive that instituted the new scheme. *USN, courtesy Don Montgomery*

cat pilots became aces in a day; by war's end 40 had "made five the hard way."

Later that summer the improved F6F-5 arrived in the fleet. Largely benefiting from spring-tab ailerons, the dash five reflected Grumman's effort to give the Hellcat the same easy, powerful roll rate of the Corsair. F6F-5s carried the bulk of the fighter load for the remaining 12 months of combat, extending air superiority from the Philippines to Okinawa and Japan itself.

Enhancing its versatility as a standard fighter and photo aircraft, the Hellcat also became the Navy and Marines' standard night fighter. F6F-3s and -5s both carried APS-4 and -6 radars in the E and N variants, with the F6F-5N becoming the most widely employed. During both the Philippines and Okinawa campaigns, land-based Marine Night Hellcats dominated the radar air war despite the presence of Army P-61 Black Widow squadrons.

Like the Wildcat, the Hellcat also logged a global war, though not to the extent of the F4F/Martlet. Two American F6F-5 squadrons flew from escort carriers during Operation Anvil-Dragoon, the Allied invasion of Southern France in August 1944, primarily providing reconnaissance and naval gunfire spotting. However, VOC-1 and VF-74 shot down eight

Replaced by the F8F Bearcat and F4U Corsair, the Hellcat didn't remain in the fleet long after World War II. Gone by late 1946, it made a brief comeback with VF-71 in 1952 as an interim replacement for the squadron's troubled F9F-5 Panther jets. VF-3 F6F-5s out of NAAS Oceana Virginia during October 1945. *Capt. Ed Baumann*

RIGHT AND OPPOSITE
The Hellcat took the war to the heart of the Japanese
Empire and also served in Europe on a comparatively
limited basis. The big Grumman fighter operated from
all types of carriers from spring 1943 until the end of
hostilities in the Pacific, 15 August 1945.

VF-16 F6F-3 is taxied forward after landing aboard
USS *Lexington* (CV-16). *USN, courtesy Stan Piet*

Luftwaffe aircraft at a time when their Pacific counterparts were preparing to tackle Japanese land-based air
in the Philippines.

By midwar, the British Royal Navy was familiar
with Grumman products and was highly pleased. By
1943 the Fleet Air Arm (FAA) still lacked home-grown
single-seat carrier fighters designed for the purpose
and quickly took to the Hellcat, originally named
Gannet. By whatever name, Britain obtained more
than 2,000 F6Fs during the war, committing them to
combat in climes as diverse as Norway and Java.

At the end of hostilities in August 1945, Britain
retained a dozen Hellcat squadrons, including nine in
the East Indies, or with the Pacific Fleet conducting
operations against Japan.

The F6F did not long remain in fleet service after
1945. The last Hellcat squadrons went away in late
1946, while night fighters remained in escort carrier
squadrons until 1947. Hellcats staged a brief comeback
when VF-71's F9F-5 Panthers were temporarily replaced
by F6F-5s from storage after the jets experienced problems in 1952. Radio-controlled F6F-5Ks were employed
that same year when the drones, carrying 1,000-pound
bombs, were dived into North Korean bridges, guided
by Douglas AD Skyraiders. The French also used Hellcats during the early stages of the Indochina war.

However, the Hellcat was almost perfectly
suited for its primary mission: taking the war to the
heart of the Japanese Empire. In that role it suc-
ceeded magnificently, ashore and afloat, by day and
by night, with the U.S. Navy, the Marines, and the
British Pacific Fleet. Seldom has any weapon been so
well crafted for its time and place in world events.

Flight deck crew respot VF-5 F6F-3s on board USS
Yorktown (CV-10) in late 1943. *Lcdr. Charles Kerlee,
courtesy CHINFO Still Photo Office*

TBF-1 Avenger comes aboard USS *Saratoga* (CV-3) as VF-12 F6F-3s are positioned forward near open elevator well. *USN, courtesy CHINFO Still Photo Office*

VF-10 F6F-3s are spotted forward on USS *Enterprise* (CV-6) catapults, ready for 1944 launch. *USN, courtesy Don Montgomery*

Vought F4U Corsair

Sleek and fast with distinctive good looks and a glamorous reputation, the F4U Corsair remains one of the most elegant aircraft of all time. Vought's design team advanced the state of the art by producing a world-class carrier fighter fully the match of any land-based adversary. Among the combatants of World War II, it was an achievement preceded only by the Mitsubishi A6M Zero series.

The Corsair is most frequently compared to the F6F Hellcat, but in fact the standard of comparison was Grumman's F4F Wildcat, which first flew in September 1937. The XF4U-1's first flight was logged two and a half years later, in May 1940, while the Hellcat's debut occurred in June 1942.

No one disputed the Corsair's enormous potential over the Wildcat. Nearly twice as heavy empty or loaded, the F4U was 80 miles per hour faster than the F4F-3 then in service, with significantly better climb and range. However, the U-Bird was also more complex to produce, required more maintenance, and suffered serious teething problems.

Vought engineer Rex Beisel conceived a low-drag airframe mated to the most powerful engine available. Pratt and Whitney's R-2800 Double Wasp was chosen for the concept designated V-166B, which incorporated advanced features such as the inverted gull wing. The gull wing achieved two benefits: the angular mating of the gull wing to the fuselage reduced drag and also permitted a conventional length landing gear for ground clearance of the 13-foot propeller.

The Navy issued the prototype contract in June 1938, with first flight two years later. By the end of 1940, the XF4U-1 had demonstrated a level speed of 404 miles per

Carrier landing problems with the early Corsairs were corrected, but too late for the "U-Bird" to fly from the CVs during initial stages of the war. Returning to the fleet in late 1944, the Corsair remained a successful carrier fighter-bomber until after the Korean War. VF-82 F4U-4 taxies for launch from USS *Randolph* (CV-15) during June 1946.
Chuck McCandless

First flight of the XF4U-1 came 29 May 1940, powered by a 2,000 horsepower Pratt and Whitney XR-2800-4 engine. Before the year ended, the new Corsair had flown 404 miles per hour, making it the fastest of all Naval fighters of the day. *Courtesy NASM*

"The Bent-Wing Bird," Vought's F4U Corsair was one of the most elegant aircraft of all time. It served well in both fighter and bomber roles. F4U-1D carries a 500-pound bomb during a factory flight c. 1944. *Author collection*

hour, an exceptional achievement for a naval fighter at a time when only the Army's new Lockheed P-38 Lightning was capable of similar performance.

Despite two accidents during the flight test program, the Bureau of Aeronautics was optimistic about the Corsair, as the Vought became known. On June 30, 1941, the Navy ordered 584 production model F4U-1s. Modifications of the original model included moving the cockpit three feet aft to permit more internal fuel, with standardized armament of six 50 caliber Colt-Browning machine guns instead of three .50s and one .30 caliber.

Squadron deliveries commenced in October 1942, much to the delight of VF-12 at San Diego. Lieutenant Commander Joseph C. Clifton's outfit began a lengthy, difficult period of taming the Corsair, learning its potential, and coping with its numerous problems. So did Tom Blackburn's VF-17 and William "Bush" Bringle's VOF-1, the Navy's first observation-fighter squadron as well as the first Marine F4U squadron, VMF-124, under Major William Gise.

There were numerous problems to solve. High-altitude engine performance was an early snag until, like the F6F, the Navy learned to pressurize the igni-

On 30 June 1941, the Navy ordered 584 production model F4U-1s. The Corsair continued in production until 1952, after more than 12,000 were built, a longevity record for piston-engine fighters. Pilot prepares for a 1942 flight in an early production model F4U-1. Canopy was later modified to one clear panel without inner framework. *Author collection*

tion harness. But carrier suitability was the Corsair's primary setback until a variety of "fixes" were implemented by the Navy squadrons with help from Vought technical representatives. Eventually VF-12, -17, and VOF-1 independently arrived at similar solutions: changing the fluid level in landing gear oleos and raising the tailwheel; adding a spoiler to the leading edge of the wing to reduce violent stall; raising the pilot's seat for improved visibility over the nose; and altering the tailhook to prevent "hook skip" on deck.

BuAer and Vought quickly agreed on standardizing the modifications, establishing a postproduction facility at San Diego. The three Navy squadrons then completed successful carrier qualifications even as

VMF-124 entered combat at Guadalcanal in February 1943. However, the conventional wisdom that the F4U was "untamable" took hold and defeated the hard work by the squadrons and company tech reps. Fighting 12 and VOF-1 were re-equipped with Hellcats before deploying to combat, and VF-17 arrived in Hawaii in summer 1943 only to learn that no F4U spare parts were available in the carrier pipeline. Replaced by an F6F squadron aboard *Bunker Hill* (CV-17), Tom Blackburn took his "Jolly Rogers" to the Solomons for land-based operations in October.

The upshot was that Corsairs would not regularly operate from American aircraft carriers until the end of 1944.

Although first delivered to Navy squadrons VF-12 and -17, the Corsair's initial combat was with VMF-124 in the Solomons during February 1943. The Marines, along with land-based VF-17, soon dominated the skies over the South Pacific islands, but not without cost. MAG-14 F4U-1A wreckage is being stripped for salvageable parts following a May 1944 landing crash in the Green Islands. Aircraft was hit by AA fire during a mission over Rabaul. *USMC, Cpl. A. Sarno*

Meanwhile, VMF-124 led the way in defeating Japanese air power in the upper Solomons. After a shaky start in the 14 February "St. Valentine's Day Massacre," Gise's Corsairs demonstrated the F4U's range and performance improvements over the F4F. Gise was killed in action, but 124 conclusively proved the bent-wing bird's ability and produced the first Corsair ace, Lieutenant Kenneth A. Walsh, who also became the first F4U pilot awarded the Medal of Honor in World War II.

By August, all eight Marine fighting squadrons in the area had re-equipped with Corsairs, and in October VF-17 as well as Lieutenant Commander W.J. "Gus" Widhelm's small night fighter squadron, VF(N)-75 also joined the battle.

With range to carry the battle to Japan's naval-air bastion on New Britain, Marine Corps and Navy Corsair squadrons flew from a succession of bases in the lower Solomons. The Armistice Day carrier strike against Rabaul featured VF-17 landing aboard *Bunker Hill* to reinforce the combat air patrol before returning to the field at Ondonga. Quite apart from the 18.5 victories claimed, the Jolly Rogers safely landed on their original ship and launched safely, without having "trapped" in almost two months.

When VF-17 completed its tour in March 1944, Lieutenant (jg) Ira Kepford was the Navy's top fighter pilot and first triple ace. By then four Marine F4U pilots each had won 20 or more victories, though Major Greg

VMF-214 F4U-1A taxies for takeoff in the Solomons, c. 1943. 214's skipper, Major Gregory "Pappy" Boyington, earned the Medal of Honor in the Corsair and became a top Corsair ace with 22 victories before he was shot down and taken prisoner. *USMC, courtesy Richard M. Hill*

Boyington, skipper of VMF-214, was a prisoner and Lieutenant Robert M. Hanson of 215 had been killed while strafing. Ken Walsh of 124 and Captain Harold Spears, also of 215, rotated back to the States.

Meanwhile, the height of irony in the Corsair's career is the fact that F4Us first flew from U.S. carriers as night fighters. In the first half of 1944, Lieutenant Commander Richard "Chick" Harmer's VF(N)-101 had radar-equipped F4U-2s aboard *Enterprise* and *Intrepid* (CV-11). Harmer's outfit had little opportunity for night combat—the deployment netted just five kills—but successfully flying dash one-style Corsairs off straight-deck carriers in the dark testified to a very high degree of pilot proficiency.

By early 1944, the British also appreciated the F4U. The Royal Navy's first Corsair squadrons had stood up in 1943 and the type entered combat from HMS *Victorious* in April 1944, during attacks on the German battleship *Tirpitz* in Scandinavian waters.

Eventually British carriers operated Corsairs in the Far East and against Japan itself. The last Victoria Cross of the war went to a Canadian flier, Sub-lieutenant Robert H. Gray, who was killed attacking an enemy warship on 9 August 1945, just six days before Japan agreed to surrender.

With 13 Corsair squadrons active at war's end, the Fleet Air Arm was a far different organization from that which began the war with one squadron of Sea Gladiators six years before. The Royal New Zealand Air Force also flew Corsairs, largely on ground-support missions in the Solomons.

Such was the demand for Corsairs that Vought could not meet production requirements. Therefore, Goodyear Aircraft built FG-1s and -1Ds at Akron,

Wartime demands precluded Vought from building all the Corsairs needed by the United States and Allied nations. Goodyear Aircraft built the Corsair as the FG and Brewster aided with its F3A version. FG-1D lands aboard a training carrier c. late 1945 or early 1946. *Mark Brown, courtesy Jeff Ethell*

Corsairs produced their share of aces—most being land-based Marines during the island-hopping campaigns of the Pacific. 1st Lt. Jeremiah J. O'Keefe beams as he indicates his score of seven victories in his F4U-1D during May 1945 on Okinawa. O'Keefe became an "ace in a day" when he downed five Val *kamikazes* on 22 April. *USMC, Beall, courtesy Don Montgomery*

Ohio, while Brewster produced F3A-1s. The latter firm, beset by poor management, shut down after delivering just 735 Corsairs, while Goodyear produced 3,808—almost one in three of all Corsair airframes built in a 12-year period.

Like a promising actor stripped of his star role and then recalled at the last minute, the Corsair returned to carriers at the end of 1944. The *kamikaze* crisis had caught the Navy unprepared for the increased demand in fighters aboard fast carriers. Combined with a reduced training program that summer, there were insufficient F6F squadrons to respond to Japan's suicide threat that emerged in the Leyte Gulf battle in October. Therefore, two Marine F4U squadrons were given short notice of deployment to Hawaii and points west. VMF-124 and -213 boarded *Essex* (CV-9) at Ulithi Atoll in December and, following a rough time with carrier procedures

and weather, met the challenge. Eight other Leatherneck squadrons followed over the next several months, flying from *Bennington*, *Wasp*, *Bunker Hill*, and *Franklin*. Additionally, two-squadron Marine air groups (one F4U, one TBM) emerged in escort carriers, specially trained for close air support of infantry.

Marine aviation's last great task of the war involved the Okinawa campaign, beginning 1 April 1945. Eventually a dozen F4U squadrons served ashore in the Tactical Air Force, taking a constant toll of conventional Japanese aircraft as well as *kamikazes*. Deployed in three Marine air groups and allied with three Army P-47 groups, the Corsairs and their Night Hellcat counterparts were on call almost constantly.

By the time Okinawa was secured in June, Corsairs had claimed 436 kills, or more than two-thirds of the TAF total. By far the most successful squadron was VMF-323, led by a pair of 24-year-

Corsairs served during World War II with the Fleet Air Arm of the Royal Navy and Royal New Zealand Air Force, as well as with the French Navy following the war. Royal Navy F4U-1B has wings clipped to 15 feet, 9 inches to accommodate it in British 16-foot hangar decks. *Author collection*

old majors: George C. Axtell and Jefferson D. Dorroh. Both the CO and exec became aces in a day on 24 April, leading the "Death Rattlers" to a total of 124.5 confirmed victories. The next leading shooters were VMF-311 (71 kills) and the Army's 19th Fighter Squadron (60 confirmed).

Summer 1945 also featured the debut of the ultimate World War II Corsair, the F4U-4. Flying both ashore and afloat, the dash four incorporated the improved R-2800-18 engine, which required a four-bladed propeller. With improved high altitude per-

formance and blazing speed of 446 miles per hour, the F4U-4 remained the Navy and Marines' standard prop fighter through the end of the Korean War.

On VJ-Day the Corsair truly had filled its promise. Credited with an 11 to 1 kill-loss ratio, the F4U emerged as a world-class fighter proven in both the Atlantic and Pacific. However, its real measure of

MGen. Marion E. Carl, USMC (Ret) was a leading Marine ace. At his retirement, he stated the F4U was "head and shoulders above its competition, on a level with the F-4 Phantom in its day." *USMC, courtesy Stan Piet*

success was the fact that on 15 August, the fast carriers operated eight F4U squadrons at war's end, while two more flew from CVEs. Such a situation would have been unthinkable less than 12 months before.

The F4U remained in production another eight years, establishing a longevity record for piston-engine fighters. In all, more than 12,200 were produced between 1940 and 1952, when the French Navy accepted its final F4U-7.

Virtually every military aviator who survived combat in a particular aircraft remains loyal to that type. But even allowing for sentiment, the Corsair remains widely regarded as "the Cadillac of propeller tailhook fighters". The sentiment was perhaps never stated more forcefully than by Marine Major General Marion E. Carl, who flew Wildcats, Corsairs, Phantoms, Crusaders, and helicopter gunships in combat. Speaking shortly before his retirement in 1973, the quiet Oregonian who became "Mr. Marine Air" summarized the F4U as "Head and shoulders above its competition, on a level with the F-4 Phantom in its day."

CHAPTER 5

Too Little or Too Late

The Navy and Marine Corps operated four other wartime fighters built by three companies, of which only the Brewster was used in combat. However, the additional VF types from Grumman and Ryan were innovative designs representing both evolutionary and "technology demonstrator" concepts that showed the way to the future.

Brewster F2A Buffalo

The Brewster Buffalo suffers from the institutionalized wisdom of half a century. Unfortunately, the shock and grief after its only wartime use by American forces at the Battle of Midway established its reputation as perhaps the worst fighter this nation has ever committed to combat. In truth, the F2A possessed some performance advantages over the F4F and was widely considered

more agile. Its greatest failing—a landing gear too fragile for carrier use—largely has been overlooked.

In studying the F2A series, it becomes obvious that there is no such thing as *the* Buffalo. The 528-strong production run was divided among eight models, only three of which were used by the U.S. Navy. In fact, less than one-third of Buffalo production went to American forces. The others were export versions for Finland, Britain, and Holland not intended for carrier use and therefore lighter and better handling.

When Fighting Three introduced it to the fleet in December 1939, the F2A-1 became the Navy's first monoplane fighter, following the Douglas TBD-1 torpedo plane by more than two years. Though only 40 miles per hour faster than the F3F-3 biplane, the Brewster (which became

North American's contemporary of the FD-1 was its straight-wing McDonnell FJ-1 Fury, of which only 33 were built, but the design led to the outstandingly successful FJ-2 through -4 swept-wing series, as well as the Air Force's F-86 Sabre. The XFJ-1 first flew 27 November 1946, and the Fury operated with only one fleet squadron, VF-5A (later VF-51). NATC FJ-1 on a test flight, c. 1947. *Courtesy NASM*

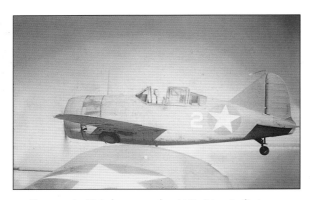

Brewster's F2A became the U.S. Navy's first mono-plane fighter, but served operationally aboard carriers in only three squadrons, VF-2, VF-3, and VS-201. The F2A did bring Navy fighters into the 300-mile-per-hour range by doing 321 miles per hour at altitude. By late 1942, they had been relegated to the training command. NAS Miami F2A-3 on a training flight in 1942. *Pete Peterson*

"Buffalo" in 1941) was a landmark design in Naval Aviation history.

However, by December 1941 the F2A was lagging; only one carrier squadron still flew it, and after a series of deck crashes, *Lexington's* VF-2 was grounded pending hostilities. Meanwhile, VMF-221 on Midway still flew Navy castoffs. The disastrous combat of 4 June began poorly for the Marines and quickly turned to hash; caught at an altitude disadvantage by superior numbers of better fighters flown by more experienced pilots, the Brewsters did well to knock down any Japanese at all, while suffering two-thirds losses. Indeed, they made an indelible impression on their opponents as Zero pilots claimed 40 "confirmed" victories and several "probables" against 19 F2As and six F4Fs. Considering the unfavorable tactical situation, it is doubtful that VMF-221 would have survived if it had flown Wildcats exclusively.

Elsewhere, Brewsters survived somewhat longer against Japan as four British Empire squadrons in Malaya and Burma boasted three Buffalo aces before

the Model 339s were destroyed or their fields overrun. The Dutch East Indies air arm similarly flew export Brewsters against the Japanese, with far fewer successes. The British Royal Navy briefly used the type in the Mediterranean as well.

In contrast, tiny Finland used its 43 Model 239s to enormous effect against the Soviets from 1941 to 1944. The Finnish Brewsters were lighter than the F2A-3, which was 20 miles per hour faster than the 239. With a very high standard of pilot proficiency and no shortage of targets, the Finns produced 35 aces in type; four with more than 20 kills apiece.

The Brewsters found a tactical home in the frigid atmosphere of the Karelian Peninsula, as the Finnish Air Force already had adopted two pair as its standard fighter formation, and was probably the only air arm beyond the U.S. Navy to train in wide-angle gunnery. Therefore, in Finnish hands the stubby Buffalo rang up a 25-1 kill-loss ratio; highly impressive even allowing for the normal error of combat claims. By then, however, Finland's alliance with Germany prevented replacements or spare parts, so the Finns re-equipped with Messerschmitt 109s and cheerfully proceeded shooting Russians at an accelerated pace.

It has taken more than 50 years, but at length the much-maligned Brewster is receiving a more objective assessment. There is even a Buffalo home page on the Internet, complete with specifications, pilot reports, and combat summaries. That the F2A was a marginal carrier aircraft is beyond dispute; that it was a successful fighter against numerically superior enemies emphasizes the danger of buying into history's conventional wisdom.

Grumman F7F Tigercat

Two Grumman cats missed combat against the Empire of the Sun, and the memory of that prospect still has their advocates licking their chops a half century later. The twin-engine XF7F-1 Tigercat first flew on 3 November 1943. With a tricycle landing gear

First flown 3 November 1943, the F7F Tigercat began service with Marine units in January 1944, primarily as a night fighter. VMF-911, a training squadron, and VMF(N)-531 were the initial outfits to operate the new fighter. However, the F7F arrived too late for World War II combat. *Rudy Arnold, courtesy NASM*

(the first ever on a Navy fighter), 420-mile-per-hour speed, and a potent battery of four 50 calibers and four 20-mm cannon, the Tigercat was packed with potential. Flying from land bases, its offensive load-out could comprise two 1,000-pound bombs or an aerial torpedo.

The dash one Tigercats were single seaters, as were the follow-on F7F-3s. But the most widely used variants were the F7F-2N and -3N, which accepted a radar operator in a claustrophobic cockpit well behind the pilot. The -4N, which was limited to merely 13 production aircraft in 1946, was the only

Designed as multimission aircraft, the Tigercats performed in a variety of roles, such as night fighter and photo recon. Envisioned for service aboard Midway-class carriers, the F7Fs never made it to the fleet, serving instead in land-based units only. Several F7F units did carrier-qualify, but never deployed aboard ship. F7F-3s are being transported from WestPac aboard a carrier, c. early 1950s. *Author collection*

Tigercat fully equipped for carrier flying, with catapult fittings and tailhook.

Squadron deliveries began in January 1944 with a training unit, VMF-911, and the Corps' first night fighter outfit, VMF(N)-531, receiving the initial batch. Five Thirty-One had inaugurated Leatherneck night fighters while flying Lockheed PV-1s in the Solomons during 1943.

Tigercats were expected to perform as multimission aircraft, and certainly they had that potential. Probably the most original "weapon" envisioned for the F7F was delivery of bats carrying thermite fuses, which would ignite when the flying rodents roosted in Japanese buildings. At war's end at least one Navy squadron was beginning to operate the type in anticipation of service aboard the Midway-class CVBs. However, VT(N)-52 was disestablished in December 1945.

After completion of some 350 aircraft in November 1946, combat finally came in Korea, largely in the night fighter and interdiction role. VMF(N)-513's land-based F7F-3Ns were credited with two of the 15 kills achieved by Marine night fighters throughout the war. The first of these, on 1 July 1951, was also the first confirmed nocturnal victory by an Allied aircraft in the "Korean Conflict."

The powerful Tigercat did not long outlive the Korean War. A utility squadron, VJ-62, last reported -3 and -4 night fighters in use at the end of March 1954. A long and successful civilian career featured aerial fire fighting in the western states during the 1960s and 1970s.

Grumman F8F Bearcat

The F8F Bearcat was the epitome of piston-engine tailhook fighters. Slightly smaller than a Wildcat, it had more horsepower under the cowling than a standard Corsair. The F8 owed its existence to a peculiar event: in 1943 Grumman test pilot Bob Hall flew a variety of Allied and captured enemy aircraft at an Allied fighter conference. He was vastly impressed with the Focke Wulf 190A's flying qualities. Upon return to Bethpage he talked to the boss, essentially telling Roy Grumman, "If we could put an R-2800 in that airframe, we'd have a world beater." Thus was born the G-58, later Bearcat, which first flew in August 1944.

With eye-watering performance, the XF8F-1 demonstrated an initial climb rate approaching 5,000 feet per minute and a top speed of 370 knots. The Navy was so enthused about the new fighter that it ordered 3,900, including 1,876 F3M-1s from General Motors. However, the abrupt end of the war resulted in cancellation of the Eastern order and reduction of Grumman deliveries to a total of 1,263 dash ones and twos.

Bearcats went to VF-19 at NAAS Santa Rosa, California, in May 1945. Returned from a highly successful Hellcat deployment, Satan's Kittens broke in the fleet's first F8F-1s and proceeded to humiliate Army fighter pilots along the West Coast on a regular basis. In one fabled episode, the skipper was challenged by the commanding officer of a nearby P-38 squadron. The bet: in a section takeoff, the Bearcat had to gain enough altitude for an overhead gunnery pass at the Lightning before the P-38 raised its wheels. Lieutenant

The epitome of piston-engine tailhook fighters, Grumman's F8F Bearcat also arrived too late for World War II combat. First squadron deliveries went to VF-19 in May 1945. F8F-1 Bearcat is seen at a "mid-Pacific base" (probably VF-19 NAS Barbers point, T.H.) c. 1945. *USN, courtesy Don Montgomery*

Commander Joe Smith actually completed a *second* overhead before the Army pilot tucked his gear in the well! Cash money changed hands.

Fighting 19 was in Hawaii when the war ended, while VF-18 was still re-forming on the West Coast. Thus the fabulous Bearcat missed its chance for combat. However, at the Cleveland Air Races in 1946, Patuxent River test pilots Bill Leonard and Butch Davenport set consecutive time-to-climb records for a combat-loaded fighter: brakes off to 10,000 feet in barely 90 seconds.

The last Bearcats were accepted by the Navy in May 1949. They lingered in squadron service until near the end of the Korean War, serving with reserve squadrons VF-859 and -921 until January 1953.

Ryan's FR-1 Fireball was the company's attempt at getting the Navy started with jet fighters, although its main propulsion was a Wright R-1820 reciprocating engine. Aided by a General Electric I-16 jet, producing only 1,600 pounds static thrust, the Fireball could maintain flight with the jet only, but could not take off without the recip. FR-1s served in the fleet with VF-1E and VF-66 (later VF-41) during the late 1940s. VF-41's Ens. Jake West made the first jet carrier landing in history when he lost power in his FR-1's recip and brought the aircraft aboard USS *Wake Island* (CVE-65) 5 November 1945. *Ryan Aircraft*

The Bearcat was arguably the finest piston-engine fighter of the world. On 20 November 1946, an F8F-1 flown by Lcdr. M.W. "Butch" Davenport, was airborne in 115 feet from a standing start and climbed to 10,000 feet in 94 seconds, a world record. Bearcats remained in the fleet until the Korean War when they were replaced by jets. F8F-2 of VF-191 (ex VF-19), comes aboard USS *Boxer* (CV-21) during 1949. *Capt. John A. Overn*

French Air Force squadrons flew Bearcats in Southeast Asia during the 1950s, while Thailand operated small numbers of F8Fs apparently as late as the 1960s.

In the civil arena, Bearcats proved fearsome contenders in closed-course air racing from the mid-1960s. Additionally, a highly modified F8F-2 captured the official world piston speed record when piloted by Darryl Greenameyer in 1969.

Ryan FR Fireball

Ryan was an unusual contender in the fighter arena, but its lone entrant was a highly unusual airplane. The XFR-1 Fireball was powered by a

The U.S. Navy's entry into jet aviation came in November 1943 when it acquired two YP-59A Bell Airacomets from the USAAF for evaluation at Patuxent River. Three YP-59Bs were later added in 1945 and 1946. Some consideration for adaptation of the 380-mile-per-hour fighter for carrier use may have been given, but no serious attempt was ever made. YP-59A BuNo 63960 (ex-42-108778) has engine panels removed during tests at Pax River during January 1944. *USN, author collection*

The Navy's plans for a jet fighter began as early as 1943 when it requested such a design from McDonnell Aircraft Corporation, the company's first Navy project. Originally designated FD-1, McDonnell's designation was changed in 1946 and the new jet became the FH-1 Phantom after its first flight 26 January 1945. The FH-1 equipped only one Navy and one Marine squadron, VF-17A (later VF-171) and VMF-122. Powered by two Westinghouse J30-WE-20 turbojets producing 1,600 pounds of thrust each, production model FD-1s are on McDonnell's flight line, c. 1946. *USN, courtesy Don Montgomery*

Wright R-1820 reciprocating engine in the nose with an anemic General Electric I-16 jet (1,600 pounds static thrust) in the tail. Additionally, because of the jet tailpipe, the Fireball possessed a tricycle landing gear, only the second carrier type so designed after the F7F.

The prototype originated with a contract on 11 February 1943, with first flight on 25 June 1944. Originally 1,200 were ordered, but by November 1945 the last of 69 production Fireballs had been delivered, all dash one models.

The original fleet squadron was VF-66, which received its first aircraft in March 1945. Quickly establishing a presence among more conventional (and better performing) types, the FR pilots reveled in the description of "One turning and one burning." They considered it grand sport to pull alongside a piston aircraft, shut down the prop, and then slowly accelerate away from the astonished witness. Top speed was rated at 400 miles per hour with both engines running; 295 miles per hour with the piston alone.

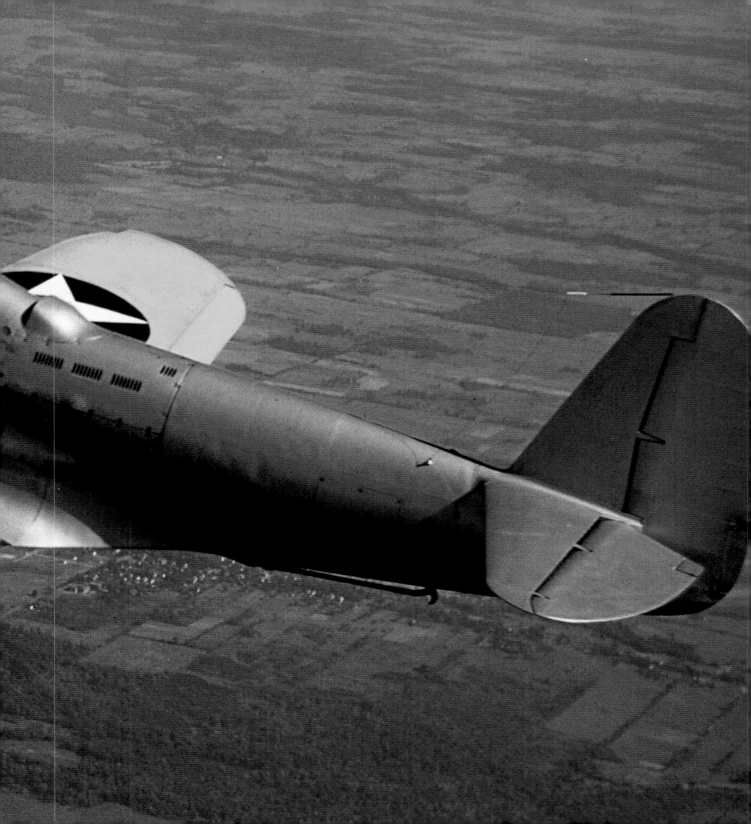

PREVIOUS: About the same time as the F4F, Bell was experimenting with modifying the Army Air Corps' P-39 Airacobra as a carrier fighter. Switching to a conventional landing gear to facilitate the tailhook and arresting gear, the XFL-1 Airabonita could not perform well enough to warrant production. This was one of the first of many examples of the failure of a land-based fighter to be converted to a successful carrier plane. *Bell, courtesy Jay Miller*

The Navy's first twin-engine fighter was to be Grumman's F5F Skyrocket, but it wound up serving only with the "Blackhawk Squadron" of comic-book fame. Only one XF5F-1 BuNo 1442, was built, powered by Wright XR-1820-40 and -42 engines with three-bladed propellers contrarotating. The Skyrocket was not the finest of Grumman's usually spectacular fighter designs. *Courtesy Grumman History Center*

Primarily operating off escort carriers, FR-1s were last reported in fleet service with VF-1E in June 1947. Though their operational life was barely two years, the Fireballs provided some badly-needed experience to the first generation of jet-propelled Naval Aviators.

Early Jets

America's first jet aircraft was Bell's YP-59 Airacomet, first flown in October 1942. Powered by two small General Electric I-16s of 1,650 pounds thrust each, the Airacomet was capable of some 400 miles per hour at 35,000 feet. The Navy received the eighth and ninth aircraft at years end, and inaugurated a generation of aviators to jet flight.

During 1943 BuAer made genuine progress toward "real" Navy jets with a contract for McDonnell

Boeing's last attempt to produce a Navy fighter was the XF8B-1, first flown 27 November 1944. Powered by a Pratt & Whitney XR-4360-10 producing 3,000 horsepower, the big 22,960-pound fighter could carry two 1,000-pound bombs in an internal bomb bay and do 432 miles per hour at altitude. The end of the war was a major factor in canceling development of the aircraft after three examples were built, one evaluated by the USAAF. *Courtesy Boeing.*

to produce the FH-1 Phantom. Like the Airacomet, the Phantom relied on two engines—Westinghouse J30s—and was first flown in January 1945. The first squadron, VF-17A, received its aircraft in July 1947. The follow-on F2H Banshee was ordered in March 1945 and from 1949 proved an exceptionally capable and long-lived aircraft.

Another wartime jet development was North American's single-engine FJ-1 Fury contracted the same month the FH first flew. In turn, the Fury was flown in late 1946 and, serving exclusively with VF-51, paved the way for the swept-wing FJ-2 through -4 series that remained in the fleet until 1962.

They Also Served

Five other naval fighters were tested during the World War II era but never entered production. These were mostly oddballs—aircraft of innovative design or unusual configuration that proved unnecessary for the war effort.

Bell's XFL-1 was essentially the Army P-39 Airacobra with a tailwheel instead of the standard tricycle configuration. Ordered in November 1938, the sleek Bell was equipped with tailhook and catapult fittings but was never seriously considered.

Another Army type was the "Sea Horse" variant of the famous P-51 Mustang. Evidently never assigned a Navy designation (presumably it would have been the FJ-1), the P-51D was, like the Bell,

given carrier modifications and tested aboard the new Essex class carrier *Shangri-La* (CV-38) in November 1944. Lieutenant Commander Robert M. Elder, a combat-experienced SBD pilot, proved the concept with a series of launches and "traps" in anticipation of the need for carrier-based fighters to escort Boeing B-29s over Japan. However, capture of Iwo Jima in March 1945 ended the Sea Horse program.

Grumman's first twin-engine fighter was the XF5F-1 Skyrocket, developed simultaneously with the P-50 version for the Army Air Force. Ordered at the same time as the Vought F4U, in 1938, the G-34 was powered by two Wright R-1820s. However, the engines proved difficult to cool sufficiently and the project was dropped in favor of the F7F Tigercat.

Undeniably the most innovative design was Vought's V-173 "flying flapjack." The unconventional airframe featured a lifting surface rather than a true fuselage with twin Pratt and Whitney R-2000s, each of 1,600 horsepower. Intended to possess a hovering capability, the Flapjack suffered a series of setbacks, but finally flew in November 1942. Partly owing to development problems, partly to concentrating on the Corsair, the Navy version XF5U-1 never flew. By then, of course, the war was over and work abruptly stopped.

Finally, a rarity appeared in midwar—a Boeing fighter. The Seattle company's previous carrier type was, of course, the popular F4B series of biplanes, but wartime urgency forced the firm to concentrate on heavy bombers. However, the XF8B-1 was contracted in May 1943, powered by Pratt and Whitney's 3,000-horsepower R-4360 driving contrarotating propellers. Three prototypes were contracted, and despite a 430-miles-per-hour top speed, the big Boeing simply was not needed by the time of its 27 November 1944 first flight.

Pearl Harbor to Tokyo Bay

CHAPTER 6

Of the 11 U.S. Navy carriers lost to enemy action from 1942 to 1945, six were directly attributable to aircraft. Only three of the six succumbed to conventional bombing or torpedo attack: *Lexington* (CV-2) at Coral Sea on 8 May 1942; *Hornet* (CV-8) in the Solomons on 26 October; and *Princeton* (CVL-23) off the Philippines two years later. The other three were escort carriers sunk by *kamikazes* between October 1944 and February 1945.

Therefore, Navy fighting squadrons did exceptionally well in their primary mission: keeping their carriers afloat. But the way the war was suddenly and unexpectedly forced upon them gave no indication of their later success.

Pearl Harbor and Aftermath

Navy F4Fs were first shot at the night of 7 December 1941, as *Enterprise* fighters tried to land at Pearl Harbor after a fruitless search for the Japanese carriers. Panicky anti-aircraft gunners opened fire on six Wildcats, with three pilots and four aircraft lost. Fighting Six would be heard from again—and often.

Across the Date Line, VMF-211's forward echelon on Wake Island was severely depleted that morning when all but five F4F-3s were destroyed in a surprise attack by Japanese Navy bombers. Over the next 16 days, Major Paul Putnam's squadron gradually eroded under the relentless weight of air and naval bombardment, and the survivors finished the fight as infantry. Before then, however, they shot down six enemy bombers, helped sink a warship, and repulsed the first landing attempt.

Beginning on 1 February, Navy squadrons struck back in a series of carrier raids against Japanese holdings in the Southwest and Central Pacific. Hit-and-run attacks on enemy bases in the Marshall and the Solomon

By early 1944, the Essex-class carriers typically embarked 36 to 40 Hellcats. Subsequently, the VF allotment was increased to 54 and finally 73 aircraft as fleet air defense became of increasing concern. Air Group Five aboard USS *Yorktown* (CV-10) during late 1943. *USN, courtesy Don Montgomery*

Lcdr. John S. "Jimmy" Thach, seen as skipper of VF-3 in 1942, developed the famed "Thach Weave" fighter tactics of World War II. Credited with 6 1/2 aerial victories while flying the F4F Wildcat, Thach rose to the rank of Admiral before retirement. *USN, courtesy Don Montgomery*

Islands were conducted by *Enterprise* and *Yorktown*, respectively. The latter had been hastily summoned from the East Coast with VF-42 relieving VF-5, which was on Neutrality Patrol in the Atlantic. Both VF-6 and VF-42 opened their victory logs during the day, and each would add to the tally during the next four months.

"Jimmy" Thach's VF-3 temporarily relieved Fighting Two in *Lexington* while the Flying Chiefs converted from Brewsters to Grummans, and therefore fought the Wildcat's first major combat. Spotted by Japanese patrol planes off New Britain on 20 February, "Lady Lex" had to cancel planned strikes against the fleet base at Rabaul. During the day the Felix squadron shot down two snoopers and 15 Mitsubishi G4M bombers, losing one pilot and two Wildcats. Naval aviation's first popularized hero of the war emerged from the interception, as Lieutenant (jg) Edward H. "Butch" O'Hare was credited with five victories.

Coral Sea

The next time *Lexington* sailed in harm's way she had Lieutenant Commander Paul Ramsey's VF-2 back aboard with F4F-3s. During the first week in May, she was teamed with *Yorktown* to contest a Japanese thrust at Port Morseby, New Guinea—gateway to northern Australia. On the 7th and 8th the

Lt. Edward H. "Butch" O'Hare was naval aviation's first World War II Medal of Honor recipient after downing five Japanese G4M (later, Betty) bombers attacking USS *Lexington* (CV-2) off New Britain 20 February 1942 while flying with Thach's VF-3. O'Hare became air group commander of CVG-6 and was killed during a night intercept mission 26 November 1943. Long believed to have been mistakenly shot down by "friendly fire," new evidence indicates he was downed by a Japanese Betty gunner. *USN, courtesy CHINFO Still Photo Office*

During the Battle of Coral Sea, 7-8 May 1942, Ens. Walter Haas, flying a VF-42 F4F, was the first Wildcat pilot to bag a Mitsubishi A6M Zero. Haas went on to become an ace in the stubby little Grumman fighter. *Courtesy Richard M. Hill*

U.S. task force clashed with three Japanese flattops in the first carrier-versus-carrier battle in history, with heavy fighter combat both days. It was the first time that Navy F4Fs tangled with Mitsubishi A6Ms, and Ensign Walter Haas of VF-42 earned the distinction of becoming the first Wildcat pilot to bag a Zero. At the end of the battle, the afternoon of the 8th, Japan had lost the light carrier *Shoho* while *Lexington* was sunk and *Yorktown* damaged. Actual aerial combat results are impossible to compute because many Japanese planes were lost to unknown causes, but VF-2 claimed 17 victories during the two days and VF-42 an even 20. However, Lex's fighters were roughly handled by Zeros, and thereafter Wildcat pilots learned to keep their speed up, using altitude to dive and zoom climb for another pass.

Tactically, the Battle of the Coral Sea was a draw, with some advantage to Japan. But the emperor's strategic aim—securing a springboard for invasion of Australia—was foiled. Moreover, because of casualties sustained by *Shokaku* and *Zuikaku*, neither of those large carriers would be present at the next battle.

Midway

Midway Atoll lies at the end of the Hawaiian chain, some 1,100 miles northwest of Oahu. Admiral Yamamoto's plan to seize Midway could not be ignored by the U.S. Pacific Fleet—a showdown was inevitable, and during the last week in May *Enterprise* and *Hornet* (CV-8) sortied together while *Yorktown*, hastily repaired, sailed separately. Armed with solid intelligence of Yamamoto's forces and plans, the remaining U.S. carriers prepared to ambush the attackers in an all-or-nothing battle for the future of Hawaii.

The battle opened early on 4 June when 107 aircraft from four Japanese carriers leveled Midway. The lone Marine fighter squadron, VMF-221, was caught at a hopeless disadvantage and lost 13 F2As plus two F4F-3s. The carrier squadrons, however, were fully equipped with new F4F-4s. Jimmy Thach was back in action with a cadre of VF-3 pilots filling most of the gaps in *Yorktown*'s seasoned VF-42. Lieutenant Jim Gray's VF-6 was well experienced in the Big E, but *Hornet*'s VF-8, and the entire air group, was new to combat.

Most of the Wildcat action occurred during two raids against *Yorktown*. However, Thach inaugurated his "beam defense" to combat while escorting "Old Yorky's" strike against the enemy flattops that morning, and proved that it worked extremely well. *Yorktown* was damaged twice, and her orphaned fighters were absorbed in *Hornet* for the rest of the battle. All four Japanese carriers were sunk by U.S. dive bombers on the 4th, and though CV-5 was finished by a submarine on the 7th, the battle ended without additional air combat. On strike escort and CAPs, the Wildcats splashed about 30 bandits in exchange for 19 F4Fs lost to all causes. Better yet, the F4F now had taken the measure of the Mitsubishi Zero.

The Navy's newest carrier at the beginning of World War II was USS *Hornet* (CV-8). *Hornet's* air group failure at the June 1942 Battle of Midway was a result of poor early-war Navy tactics and the inability of Hornet Air Group to complete its training. CV-8 steams out of Pearl Harbor c. June or July 1942. *USN, courtesy Don Montgomery*

Guadalcanal

For the remainder of the year, and into early 1943, the F4F-4 was the only fighter available to the Navy and Marine Corps. When the Guadalcanal campaign began in late August, Marine squadrons were committed as they became available, beginning with VMF-223 and shortly thereafter with -224. Dependent upon coastwatchers to provide the 45 minutes' notice to take off and climb to intercept altitude, the Wildcat pilots literally lived and died by the radio link to observers in the northern Solomons.

The F4F's simple, rugged airframe and reliable Pratt and Whitney engine kept the "Cactus Air Force" in business. Though derided for its sluggish climb and heavier weight than the -3, the F4F-4's potent six-gun armament proved more than adequate to destroy Japanese twin-engine bombers, and the result was the first batch of major American aces in the war: Marine pilots John L. Smith, Marion Carl, Joe Foss, and Bob Galer being the most notable. The 1942–43 battles also generated no fewer than eight

F4F Medal of Honor recipients—more than any other single-engine aircraft in American history.

Guadalcanal also was responsible for the third and fourth carrier battles: Eastern Solomons in August and Santa Cruz in October. The first occurred barely two weeks after the initial landings, when the Japanese attempted to retake the island. *Enterprise* and *Saratoga* opposed three enemy flattops, as "Sara's" SBDs and TBFs sank IJNS *Ryujo* on 24 August. However, *Shokaku* and *Zuikaku* pummeled Task Force 61 and damaged The Big E. In turn, VF-5 and -6 shot down about 30 raiders and both sides withdrew.

Two months later, the odds had not improved for the U.S. Navy. *Enterprise* and *Hornet* were left to repel the most ambitious Japanese plan to end the Guadalcanal bloodletting, as the campaign had turned into attrition warfare that drained both sides.

The Imperial Army and Navy, in a rare example of cooperation, attempted a joint plan to tie up American seapower while allowing large numbers of troops to get ashore. U.S. Navy forces were depleted with the loss of *Wasp* (CV-7) to a Japanese submarine in September, and luckless *Saratoga* was again licking torpedo wounds.

The adversaries exchanged simultaneous air strikes on 26 October, with damage to *Junyo* and *Shokaku* by American dive bombers.

Meanwhile, successive enemy strike groups assailed the U.S. task force, aided by heavy clouds, which tended to negate the American advantage of radar. Aichi dive bombers and Nakajima torpedo planes inflicted mortal damage on *Hornet*, which was abandoned and finished off by the Japanese that night. *Enterprise*, meanwhile, sustained bomb damage that jammed her aft elevator. Her own planes and most of *Hornet's* orphans got aboard, thanks to the uncanny skill of LSOs Robin Lindsay and Jim Daniels.

The two FitRons, Lt. Cdr. Jim Flatley's new VF-10 and Mike Sanchez's VF-72, gave as good as they got. But the F4F-4's limited ammunition capacity proved a factor in the battle. Skillful aviators such as Lt. Stanley "Swede" Vejtasa and Ens. George Wrenn splashed multiple bandits over the task force, then watched in frustration while more bandits attacked after the Grummans went "ammo minus." Twenty-three Wildcats were lost to all causes while destroying at least 33 enemy aircraft. In pure fighter combat the F4Fs and Zeros probably broke even.

Air combat continued on a weekly if not daily basis until February 1943, when Japan finally acknowledged the brutal reality that was Guadalcanal. A successful evacuation of surviving Imperial Army troops was achieved that month, and both sides paused to count their losses and plan for the future.

The Solomons Air Campaign

Based on tests of an A6M2 retrieved from the Aleutians in summer 1942, an air intelligence summary was prepared at NAS San Diego that distilled the wisdom of combat experience:

The Zero fighter, because of its low wing loading, has superior maneuverability to all our present service type aircraft. It is necessary to maintain a speed of over 300 miles per hour, indicated, to successfully combat this plane. In developing tactics against the Zero, cognizance should be taken of two facts:

1. The slow rate of roll of the Zero at high speeds
2. Inability of the Zero engine to continue operating under negative acceleration.

This summary, in context with combat experience, set the stage for Navy and Marine Corps fighter tactics for the rest of the war. Combined with the four-plane division of two pair operating semi-independently, the Thach Weave became doctrine in the naval service and survives today in the form of "loose deuce" jet tactics.

In August 1943—12 months after the Guadalcanal landings—naval fighter strength in the Solomons had expanded dramatically. All eight Marine FitRons in the South Pacific had re-equipped with Corsairs while two Navy squadrons flew Hellcats and four retained Wildcats.

There were large-scale, hard-fought air battles over Guadalcanal and the lower Solomons during summer 1943, but the net result was depletion of Japan's carefully hoarded surplus of trained carrier aircrews. Representative of these actions was the Medal of Honor performance turned in by 1st Lt. James E. Swett of VMF-221. On 7 April 1943 he intercepted a flight of eight Vals among many other raiders striking U.S. shipping around Tulagi. Separated from his wingman, Swett attacked alone and shot down seven Aichis, then emptied his remaining ammunition into the eighth. Shot up by enemy gunners and zealous "friendly" AA crews, he ditched his battered Wildcat and was rescued by solicitous sailors.

That fall, Commander Aircraft Solomons (ComAirSols) began coordinating American and New Zealand squadrons in a series of raids against the Japanese naval-air complex on Rabaul, New Britain. Rabaul, with five airfields and a fine harbor, was more than 500 miles north of Guadalcanal but advanced bases had been won in the New Georgia area.

In concert with Fifth Air Force bombers from the New Guinea command of Lt. Gen. George Kenney, AirSols began wearing down Rabaul's defenses. At the tip of the Solomons spear were increasing numbers of F4Us, which first appeared in February as Major William E. Gise's VMF-124 introduced the Corsair to combat. That August all eight Marine FitRons in combat were flying the elegant Voughts, and their first ace was 1st Lt. Kenneth A. Walsh, a "mustang" who had earned his wings of gold as a private in 1935.

The Rabaul battles peaked in November, when carrier raids were launched on the 5th and 11th. The latter involved the new *Essex* (CV-9) and *Bunker Hill* (CV-17) with new Hellcats embarked. *Saratoga* with light carrier *Princeton* also were involved, fighting a day-long series of battles in which more than 100 shootdowns were claimed. Land- and carrier-based F6Fs featured prominently, as did the Corsairs of VF-17, which had been kicked off *Bunker Hill* (CV-17) when Lt. Cdr. Tom Blackburn learned no F4U spare parts were available.

Rabaul finally was beaten into submission in early 1944, left to languish in the backwater of the Pacific War. By then the crop of new names had flourished in the newspapers and faded: Boyington, Hanson, Aldrich, Spears, and so many more.

The Night Fighters

At this time, Navy and Marine Corps aviation was expanding its capabilities to the point of land- and carrier-based night fighters. VMF(N)-531, the Corps' first nocturnal squadron, flew radar-equipped PV-1 Venturas in the Solomons under Lt. Col. John D. Harshberger. Lt. Cdr. W.J. Widhelm's VF(N)-75 also served there with F4U-2s.

At sea off the Gilberts, Butch O'Hare pioneered carrier night fighters from *Enterprise*, using two F6F-3 Hellcats controlled by the radar operator in a TBF-1C. The "bat team" arrangement worked well the night of 26 November as the Avenger shot down two enemy bombers, but O'Hare's talents were lost to the Navy when he disappeared—probably the victim of an anonymous Betty gunner.

Subsequently night fighters became fully integrated into carrier air groups and operated with increasing success. Lt. Cdr. R.E. "Chick" Harmer took VF(N)-101 aboard *Enterprise* with a separate detachment in *Intrepid* (CV-11) for the first half of 1944. The nocturnal Corsairs operated in relative safety—surely the height of irony after F4Us were declared "unsafe" for daytime use—but had relatively little opportunity to ply their trade. A lone Marine squadron, VMF(N)-532, flew F4U-2s in the Central Pacific.

However, dedicated F6F night squadrons soon appeared, most notably VF(N)-76 under Lt. Cdr. Evan P. Aurand. Operating in four-plane "dets" aboard several fast carriers, Pete Aurand's outfit plus VF(N)-77 and -78 provided both offensive and defensive capabilities between dusk and dawn.

Eventually two SBD veterans showed the Navy the full potential of night carriers. Lt. Cdr. William I. Martin trained VT-10 to a high standard of night attack aboard *Enterprise* in early 1944, and that fall Cdr. Turner F. Caldwell led a two-squadron night air group from *Independence* (CVL-22). VF(N)-41 produced two aces while bagging 46 enemy aircraft in a cruise that ended in early 1945. By then, the VFN dets aboard big-deck carriers had been absorbed into the resident fighter squadrons for greater coordination.

Admirals Marc A. Mitcher (upper), William F. Halsey (above), and Raymond A. Spruance (left) were the Navy's premier carrier admirals throughout the war in the Pacific. *All photos USN, courtesy Don Montgomery*

However, the tireless Bill Martin returned with his own Night Air Group 90 in late 1944, remaining aboard The Big E until she was *kamikazed* in May 1945. *Saratoga* and the brand-new *Bon Homme Richard* (CV-31) also operated night air groups, though Sara's three-squadron experiment was violently shortened when she took suicide damage at Iwo Jima that might well have sunk a lesser ship. Meanwhile, VF(N)-90 and -91 took the night away from Japanese airmen over Okinawa and the Home Islands.

The Marines' own Night Hellcats were committed to the Philippines and Okinawa campaigns, largely replacing Army P-61 Black Widows in both arenas. Three Leatherneck squadrons at Okinawa were especially successful, destroying 69 airborne hostiles between April and August. Masterkiller among them was Maj. Marion Magruder's VMF(N)-533 with 35 victories including six by Capt. Bob Baird, the service's only night ace.

The European War

In November 1942, as the Guadalcanal campaign neared its climax, America's second offensive of the war got underway off the coast of Africa. Operation Torch, the Allied invasion of French Morocco, was supported by a mixed air group aboard *Ranger* (CV-4) plus three escort carriers.

While Army troops focused on the main landing area around Casablanca, naval aviators flew air superiority missions and supported the infantry. The Vichy French government, officially allied with Nazi Germany since 1940, opposed the Anglo-American landings and forced traditional allies into combat. The majority of air-to-air action was logged by Lt. Cdr. Tommy Booth's VF-41 and Jack Raby's VF-9, both embarked in *Ranger*. Over a three-day period, 8-11 November, their Wildcats shot down 25 aircraft (including two British planes) in exchange for five losses. Total F4F casualties were 25, including 14 to

noncombat causes owing to a low standard of readiness. However, the pilots learned much and some of them became standouts in the Pacific.

Almost a year later *Ranger* was back in action in vastly different climes, operating with the Royal Navy north of the Arctic Circle. Her mission was Operation Leader, an antishipping strike on the port of Bodo, Norway, on 4 October 1943. The Red Rippers were still aboard, redesignated VF-4, and their white-and-gray F4Fs provided strike escort and ForceCAP. Two German snoopers were shot down near the task force; when the squadron deployed in *Essex* and *Bunker Hill* in 1945 it became the only Navy unit to score kills against three Axis powers.

Carrier aviation's third and last notable action in Europe was Anvil-Dragoon, the August 1944 landing in Southern France. Two U.S. F6F squadrons were engaged, as were British Hellcats operating from CVEs. Lt. Cdrs. W.F. "Bush" Bringle (VOF-1) and H.B. "Brink" Bass (VF-74) flew from *Tulagi* (CVE-69) and *Kasaan Bay* (CVE-72) respectively. Between them they shot down eight Luftwaffe aircraft but were more urgently involved in armed reconnaissance and spotting naval gunfire. VOF-1 shortly was redesignated VOC-1 and rushed to the Pacific in time for the Philippines operation, flying FM-2 Wildcats.

The Fast Carrier Task Force

In January 1944, Vice Adm. Marc Mitscher, Naval Aviator Number 33, assumed command of the Fast Carrier Task Force. Composition of the FCTF varied somewhat but the basic organization was well established: three or four (ultimately five) task groups each built around two CVs and two CVLs, plus battleships, cruisers, and destroyers in the escorting screen. With a sound fighter direction doctrine for radar control and efficient communications, the fast carriers were virtually immune from conventional air attack.

Lt. Hamilton McWhorter of VF-9 became the first Hellcat ace, and also became the first Hellcat double ace. McWhorter ended his combat days with 12 victories. *USN, courtesy Richard M. Hill*

VF-16's Ens. E. Ralph Hanks became the Hellcat's first "ace in a day" when he shot down five confirmed Japanese aircraft in his initial combat off Tarawa 23 November 1943. Hanks was flying from USS *Lexington* (CV-16). *USN, courtesy Richard M. Hill*

By this time an Essex-class carrier typically embarked 36 to 40 Hellcats, or double the standard F4F complement two years before. Subsequently the VF allotment increased to 54 and finally 73 aircraft as fleet air defense increasingly became a concern.

Mitscher's force was alternately known as Task Force 38 or 58, depending on whether Adm. William F. Halsey (Third Fleet) or Raymond A. Spruance (Fifth Fleet) commanded a particular operation. In either case, operating procedures were identical.

The Fast Carriers supported the Kwajalein landings in January, then began a series of hard-hitting raids against Japan's vulnerable outposts. The most notable of these was the strike against Truk Atoll in the Caroline Islands, 17 February 1944. As the empire's largest fleet base outside home waters, Truk was filled with shipping and guarded by airfields. Its reputation was such that, upon hearing of the plan, VF-9 skipper Phil Torrey said, "My first impression was to jump overboard."

A spectacular dawn fighter sweep erupted into "a Hollywood war" with Hellcats, Zeros, and Rufe floatplanes trading tracer fire. The 70 F6Fs eventually won air superiority, allowing SBDs and TBFs to attack anchored shipping and destroy airfield facilities. Among those adding to their scores were VF-9's Lieutenant Hamilton McWhorter, already the first Hellcat ace who also became the type's first double ace, and Lt. (jg) Alex Vraciu of VF-6 who ran his score to nine. Carrier aviators claimed 124 shootdowns while losing 25 planes to enemy action.

Truk was revisited on 29 April, where Hellcat pilots were credited with another 58 victories. Regardless of the accuracy of combat claims, it was now clear that Mitscher's force could sail almost anywhere it wished and establish air superiority in one or two days. That prospect did not bode well for Imperial Japan.

The Turkey Shoot

In June 1944, west of the Marianas Islands, 14 American carriers fought nine Japanese flattops in the greatest carrier battle of all time. With 400 Hellcats embarked in Mitscher's ships, experienced and confident fighter pilots knew that the Imperial Navy could not ignore the threat to Saipan and Guam. In American hands, the Marianas would provide bases for long-range bombers within reach of Tokyo itself.

From the first fighter sweep on the afternoon of 11 June, enemy opposition was plentiful. However, Japan's numerical advantage in land- and carrier-based aircraft was more than offset by the qualitative superiority of U.S. Navy planes and aircrews. When the carrier phase of the battle opened on the 19th, Mitscher's staff had no doubts as to the outcome— they were going to record a decisive victory in the first carrier battle in almost two years.

During the day the Japanese Mobile Fleet launched four major strikes against Task Force 58 totaling 300 sorties or more, while planes on Guam and Saipan also were available. The three largest raids were intercepted well out and chopped up piecemeal. The other, limited to just 14 planes that reached the target area, were involved in a brief skirmish. While the "big boys" in the Essex carriers did most of the shooting (VF-15 alone claimed nearly 70 kills), the CVLs also were heard from, especially *Princeton's* VF-27.

Though Vice Adm. Ozawa's carriers were not seen by American aviators this day, his flagship *Taiho* and veteran *Shokaku* were sent to the bottom by U.S. submarines.

At sunset, TF 58 fliers were credited with 380 aerial victories—the all-time American record. During the "Great Marianas Turkey Shoot" six Hellcat pilots had shot down five or more planes apiece while total task force aircraft losses were under 30.

The following afternoon more than 200 of Mitscher's planes caught up with the fleeing Japanese at

The Navy's top ace of World War II was Cdr. David McCampbell, CAG 15, who ended the war with 34 victories and the Medal of Honor. *USN, courtesy Don Montgomery*

extreme range. They sank *Hiyo* and two oilers and damaged several other ships, losing 20 planes in combat. However, the long flight back to the darkened task force resulted in 70 aircraft lost to fuel exhaustion or deck crashes. But Japan was finished as a carrier navy.

To the Philippines

Hellcat pilots found good hunting elsewhere in June and July, most notably in a series of hard-fought combats over Iwo Jima. Strikes also were flown against the Japanese-controlled island of Formosa, but in October the greatest naval battle of World War II was conducted in conjunction with America's return to the Philippines.

Preliminary strikes began in September, but the Battle of Leyte Gulf on 24-25 October involved air, surface, and submarine action that stretched well

"The Forgotten Men" are the landing signal officers who brought the Navy's combat pilots and air crew safely back aboard the carriers. USS *Lexington* (CV-16) LSO, Ltjg. "Bud" Deering, guides a plane aboard Lex during the Marshalls and Gilberts operations, c. November 1943. Assistant LSO, Lt. Butler, observes from behind. *USN, courtesy CHINFO Still Photo Office*

"The Indispensable Men" were the enlisted mechs who kept the combat planes flying. Aviation Machinist Mates aboard Lex work on a VF-16 F6F-3 R-2800 engine between strikes against Mili and Kwajelein, c. early December 1943. *USN, Capt. Edw. M. Steichen, courtesy CHINFO Still Photo Office*

beyond the Leyte landing area. Major enemy fleet units were attacked west of the Philippines with very little aerial opposition, and the next day Japan's four seaworthy carriers were sunk off the northeast coast of Luzon. Meanwhile, heavy raids from Japanese army and navy aircraft pummeled the American task groups, resulting in 270 shootdowns on the 24th.

That day a bold enemy dive bomber pilot sank *Princeton*, the last American fast carrier lost in combat. Naval aviation's last Medal of Honor of the war was cinched that morning as Cdr. David McCampbell, CAG15 in *Essex*, shot down nine fighters in one mission. He remained the Navy's top-scoring ace of all time with a total of 34 confirmed victories. A quiet *Intrepid* pilot of VF-18 ran his score to 23 as Lt. Cecil Harris moved into the second spot.

From 10 October to 30 November, 22 Hellcat squadrons claimed 1,300 aerial victories. Four squadrons each claimed more than 100: VF-15 (*Essex*), -18 (*Intrepid*), -19 (*Lexington*), and -20 (*Enterprise*).

By the end of December 1944, the reconquest of the Philippines was assured, with Marine F4Us and SBDs supporting the ground troops. Meanwhile, Naval Aviation raised its sights to the next major target: Tokyo.

Okinawa and Japan

The Philippine campaign had reversed a two-year immunity of American carriers to Japanese air attack. At a stroke in Leyte Gulf, *kamikazes* had forced a rethinking of task force air defense, and immediate measures were taken. First, Essex-class air groups were increased to 73 fighters, forcing part of each bombing and torpedo squadron to be "beached." But second, because of a cutback in training earlier that year, the Navy had insufficient fighter pilots to meet the crisis.

Enter the Marines.

Just before the end of 1944, two Marine Corps F4U squadrons reported aboard *Essex* at Ulithi Atoll. Lt. Col. William Millington took VMF-124 and -213 to the fleet in a hasty interim move to hold the line until more Navy pilots became available. Eventually eight more Leatherneck squadrons joined fast carrier air groups, and they made notable contributions. However, they also sustained serious operational losses to poor weather and the unfamiliar carrier environment.

It was, however, long-delayed vindication for the "U-Bird." Since VF-17 had been beached from *Bunker Hill* in 1943, the Bureau of Aeronautics finally had acknowledged the reality that Tom Blackburn's crew, plus Joe Clifton's VF-12, had tamed the fearsome Corsair.

Another development in early 1945 was the creation of bombing-fighting (VBF) squadrons. With 73 aircraft and 110 or more pilots in existing VF units, the administrative workload was onerous. Therefore, fighter squadrons were divided with the executive officer assuming command of the VBF unit. Tactically there was no difference, as both squadrons flew the same aircraft aboard ship, though newly-created VBF outfits increasingly were equipped with F4Us.

Task Force 38 launched major strikes against French Indochina in mid-January 1945, reestablishing the Allied presence there after nearly three years. The expected Japanese fleet units were not found, though a disarmed French cruiser was sunk and a 14th Air Force B-24 was shot down after it unaccountably fired at Marine Corsairs.

Four weeks later, on 16 February, TF 38 brought the war to the enemy capitol. The first anniversary of the Truk raid was marked by poor weather, which failed to interfere with sustained combat as carrier pilots claimed 270 confirmed kills. Of the 16 air groups involved, seven were involved in their first-ever missions. However, they coped well. Air Group 80 from *Hancock* (CV-19)—in combat since Novem-

The wreckage of an F6F-3 Hellcat burns on Ondonga Airfield on New Georgia Island of the Solomon chain. The aircraft crashed and hit a berthing area on 10 December 1943. Note the tents and cots amidst the wreckage. *US Navy, courtesy Don Montgomery*

ber—claimed a record 71 shootdowns during the day under the leadership of CAG Albert O. "Scoop" Vorse, a veteran of the 1942 battles. The next day's pace was considerably subdued, with "only" 97 claims, but the Hellcats and Corsairs would be back.

Next on the agenda was support of the Iwo Jima occupation, 750 miles south of Tokyo. Tokyo and environs were revisited on 18 March, the last significant action before the Okinawa invasion on April Fool's Day.

Thus began perhaps the most intensive period of the Pacific air war. Between 1 April and 23 June,

TF 38 was engaged on a daily basis with close air support, combat air patrol, and periodic strikes at Japan. Carrier-based Hellcats and Corsairs shot down more than 1,000 enemy aircraft while the Marines of the shore-based Tactical Air Force (TAF) bagged 600 more.

A dozen Marine F4U squadrons dominated the TAF, with Leatherneck aviators' biggest day of the war on 12 April when they claimed 87 victories. The most successful TAF squadron was VMF-323, led by 24-year-old Maj. George Axtell whose "deadly passel

Memorial services are held on USS *Franklin's* (CV-13) hangar deck to honor her 724 dead and 265 wounded crewmen. On 19 March 1945, *Franklin* became the most severely damaged Fast Attack carrier to survive the war when she was struck by two bombs from a Japanese Judy bomber which set off devastating hangar and flight deck fires. *US Navy courtesy CHINFO Still Photo Office*

of kids" scored 124.5 kills. By this time, all-Marine air groups aboard CVEs were in combat, supporting their infantry counterparts with Corsairs and night-fighter or photo Hellcats.

Indicative of the F4U's growing acceptance was *Bunker Hill's* Air Group 84, with VF-84 plus VMF-221 and -451 in addition to the Helldivers and Avengers. Under Cdr. Roger Hedrick (formerly of VF-17), the "Wolf Gang" conclusively proved the Corsair as a carrier fighter-bomber

before the ship was severely damaged by suiciders on 11 May. Another all-Corsair fighter outfit was Air Group 10, riding *Intrepid* during a third combat deployment after flying Wildcats and Hellcats from *Enterprise.* Both VF and VBF-10 deployed with F4U-1Ds and, following return to the West Coast for repairs, returned with F4U-4s just before the war's end.

While the *kamikazes* had not been defeated—they remained a threat—the flattops proved up to

Two VMF-351 FG-1D Corsairs and a VMTB-132 TBM-3E Avenger warm up their engines aboard USS *Cape Glouster* (CVE-109) during operations off Kyushu, Japan, 8 September, 1945. *US Navy, courtesy Don Montgomery*

the challenge. No fast carrier was sunk by suicide attack, and most of those damaged by "zoot suiters" returned to combat. The major exceptions were *Enterprise, Franklin,* and *Bunker Hill.*

With conclusion of the Okinawa campaign in June, the fast carriers turned their full attention to Japan proper. During this period the Navy's premier fighter team emerged from a series of strikes and CAPs: Lt. Eugene Valencia's VF-9 division flying from *Yorktown* (CV-10) and *Lexington* (CV-16). The four pilots splashed 43 planes, with Valencia raising his wartime total to 23.

During July and August, Third Fleet bombed and shelled Japanese naval, air, and industrial targets on Honshu. Aerial opposition dropped dramatically (no Navy squadrons scored in the last three weeks of June) as Tokyo hoarded its resources against the expected invasion in November.

Aerial combat remained surprisingly rare in the first half of August as carrier fighters averaged merely two or three victories per day. However, on 15 August the morning strike groups were just crossing inland when the word came: Japan had agreed to unconditional surrender. But some Japanese pilots either did not receive the cease-fire order or chose to ignore it. *Yorktown's* VF-88 fought the last dogfight of the war, claiming nine for the loss of four. Up until 2:00 P.M., TF 38 splashed 34 enemy planes, the final victory going to *Belleau Wood's* (CVL-24) VF-31, the leading Independence-class FitRon.

Thus ended Naval Aviation's fighter contribution to the Second World War. From a technical and numerical deficit in 1941–42, through the massive buildup to parity in 1943 and the steamroller campaign across the world's greatest ocean in 1944–45, Wildcats, Hellcats, and Corsairs were ever in the vanguard of the thrust that ended only when it reached Tokyo Bay.

Grumman's World War II cats pose for a family photo during a 1996 flight over San Diego, California. Leading the formation is an F6F-5 Hellcat, followed by an F8F-2 Bearcat and F7F-3 Tigercat. *LCDR Tom Twomey*

 # Appendix

Fighter Type	Produced*	Remaining 1995	(Flyable)
Grumman F4F/ Eastern FM Wildcat	7,905	41	(16)
Grumman F6F Hellcat	12,275	28	(9)
Grumman F7F Tigercat	364	14	(6)
Grumman F8F Bearcat	1,263	31	(13)
Vought/Goodyear/ Brewster Corsair	12,570	88	(35)
Totals	34,377	198	(79)

* Production figure includes postwar; Brewster F2A was prewar.

One in 173 remains, according to "Warbird Watch" of June 1995.

By comparison, there were 301 P-51 Mustangs, 74 Curtiss P-40s, 50 Republic P-47s, and 31 Lockheed P-38s.

A beautifully restored FM-2 Wildcat survived the war to thrill air show crowds with the sight of the deadly little fighter.
Author collection

Bibliography

Lundstrom, John. *The First Team*. Annapolis, Md.: Naval Institute Press, 1984.

———.*The First Team and the Guadalcanal Campaign*. Annapolis, Md.: Naval Institute Press, 1994.

Thruelsen, Richard. *The Grumman Story*. New York: Praeger, 1976.

Tillman, Barrett. *Corsair: The F4U in WW II and Korea*. Annapolis, Md.: Naval Institute Press, 1979.

———. *Hellcat: The F6F in WW II*. Annapolis, Md.: Naval Institute Press, 1979.

———.*Wildcat: The F4F in WW II*. Annapolis, Md.: Naval Institute Press, 1990.

———. *U.S. Navy Fighter Squadrons in WW II*. North Branch, Minn.: Specialty Press, 1997.

U.S. Navy. *United States Naval Aviation, 1910–1970*. Washington, D.C.: Government Printing Office, 1971.

Wagner, Ray. *American Combat Planes*. New York: Doubleday, 1968.

Many surviving World War II fighters have entered the unlimited-class air racing scene in the United States. W.R. Laidlaw flies his F4U-7 in the U.S. Cup Race held at San Diego, California, 18 July 1971. *Robert L. Lawson*

This F6F-3 BuNo 66237, of VF-21, was ditched off San Diego, 12 January 1944, and recovered from the Pacific Ocean in October 1970. Restored, it is now on display at the San Diego Aerospace Museum. *Robert L. Lawson*

INDEX